PREACHING ON
THE HOLY SPIRIT

D0873083

Hendrickson Preaching Series

PREACHING ON THE HOLY SPIRIT

D. W. CLEVERLEY FORD

HENDRICKSON
PUBLISHERS
PEABODY, MASSACHUSETTS 01961-3473

First published 1990 by Mowbray, a Cassell imprint, London

PREACHING ON THE HOLY SPIRIT

© D. W. Cleverley Ford 1990

Hendrickson Publishers, Inc., Edition 1994

ISBN 1-56563-046-7

Reprinted by arrangement with Mowbray,
an imprint of Cassell plc, London.

Printed in the United States of America

All rights reserved.

No part of this book may be used or reproduced in any manner
whatsoever without prior written permission.

CONTENTS

ACKNOWLEDGEMENTS

The Editor of *The Expository Times*, the Reverend Dr C. S. Rodd, has very kindly given his permission for the sermon entitled 'New Life Through the Spirit', already published in the May 1987 number of that journal, to be reprinted here. I am grateful.

And once again I have to thank Miss Barbara Hodge at Canterbury for the painstaking work she has done in preparing my handwritten manuscript for the publishers. I am fortunate to have her expertise.

I would also like to express my appreciation and the encouragement given me by Ruth McCurry, newly appointed Religious Editor of Cassell, the publishers, to finish this book on the Holy Spirit for Mowbray.

D. W. CLEVERLEY FORD
Lingfield 1989

INTRODUCTION

Throughout the writing of this book, *Preaching on the Holy Spirit*, I have been at pains to keep in mind the average churchgoer. I have not written for theologians, not even for theological students or Church historians. I am far from being indifferent to theology, and Church history is an abiding interest, but, for many years, I was a parish priest and dare to think that I know something about people, including Church people. And when it comes to the subject of this book, the Holy Spirit, my guess is that, for the most part, their knowledge ceases where it ceases in the Apostles' Creed, 'I believe in the Holy Spirit'—full stop. And when this limited confession is expanded in the Nicene Creed, now repeated by Christian congregations more than ever—'We believe in the Holy Spirit, the Lord, the giver of life, who proceeds from the Father and the Son. With the Father and the Son he is worshipped and glorified. He has spoken through the prophets'—I fear the resultant enlightenment is meagre.

But does this matter? I believe it matters greatly because as the Creed testifies the Holy Spirit is the Lord, the giver of life, the life shared by God the Father and God the Son in which sharing, or communion, we are able to join by reason of the same Holy Spirit. Hence the benediction which is probably the one other liturgical phrase mentioning the Holy Spirit to 'ring a bell' with most churchgoers—'The grace of our Lord Jesus Christ, and the love of God, and the fellowship (sharing) of the Holy Spirit be with us all evermore'. The Holy Spirit is concerned with experience, our experience as men and women, our experience of God in Christ. There is no part of experience which the Holy Spirit does not touch. This is why in writing this book I am in no way offering something rarefied and impractical, but rather broad and down-to-earth.

There are stories about people and events in this book because these are the points at which attention is grasped for a subject, not least preaching on the Holy Spirit. Understandably therefore I have drawn to some extent on the Acts of the Apostles, which might almost be called the Acts of the Holy Spirit. Here St Luke tells us what the Holy Spirit *does* rather more than what the Holy Spirit *is*, and this is where we are advised to start and possibly even continue. So preaching on the Holy Spirit must be practical and not theoretical, lit up if possible with illustrations from contemporary life.

Some readers may be disappointed that I have not given much attention to the modern Charismatic Movement. I know about it, I appreciate it, and I rejoice at the new life it has brought to many churches. There can be no life apart from the Holy Spirit, but life is caught rather than taught, yet at some stage, and, especially in a responsible pastoral ministry, there must be teaching, and it needs to be geared to what those who hear are able to receive. This is my apology to those who may complain that my book lacks Pentecostal fervour.

Some of my readers will use what I have written for preaching, I hope they will, but not slavishly to copy it—some sermons are too long for that anyway—but rather to operate as a spark for ideas and lines of approach able to be processed to meet particular preaching occasions.

D.W.C.F.

1

GOD IN EXPERIENCE

You will be baptized with the Holy Spirit, and within the next few days. Acts 1.5 (NEB)

1. *The command to wait*

This is Whitsunday, or Pentecost, as we now call it, so I would like you to imagine eleven men ten days before it dawned. They are pacing up and down. No, the New Testament does not specifically say so but they had been instructed to wait about, and we all know how difficult that is. Picture the departure lounge at Gatwick when the aircraft flights are delayed! Think of yourself in the dentist's waiting room! These eleven men pacing up and down were the eleven apostles told to wait for baptism with the Holy Spirit within the next few days. What did they expect? What did they fear? No, I cannot see them sitting still with folded hands! They were people of flesh and blood like you and me. What is the Holy Spirit anyway? What would you say?

And they grew tired of waiting. They wanted to be up and doing. They reckoned that it was up to them to get the Church organized—an urge never absent for long in ecclesiastical circles. After all they were an apostle short. Judas had committed suicide. They must make up the number and proceeded to draw up a short list of possible candidates. Can you blame them? But they went about making the final selection in a very strange way. They threw a dice, or something very like throwing a dice; and, as the Authorized Version of Acts, chapter 1 quaintly writes up the story, 'the lot fell on Matthias; and he was numbered with the eleven apostles'. Was it a blunder? We never hear of Matthias again! Peter, not surprisingly, was behind all this activity. He couldn't wait. He couldn't sit still. He wasn't that sort. He had to be 'up and doing'. But there are times when, if we don't wait, we miss what we most need. And what Pentecost stands for is one of them.

1

2. *The epoch-making day*

And then it happened. Ten days after the Ascension of Jesus into heaven all the apostles were together in one place when suddenly, and without warning, they experienced God strikingly. It was like the noise of a strong, driving wind, and like tongues of fire settling on each one of them. How else was it possible to put what took place that day into mere words? This, then, was the baptism with the Holy Spirit of which the Risen Christ had spoken. All very strange, but this much was crystal clear—the Holy Spirit is the living God as we experience him. This is who he is.

And now look at the event on the page of world history. It was epoch-making. The word is not too strong. There had been in the story of God's dealings with his people all that which is covered by the Old Testament, the law and the prophets. Then there was that utterly unique occasion when Jesus was baptized by John in the river Jordan and he, the Son, became the *Man of the Spirit*. And when his ministry of living, dying, rising again and ascending to heaven was completed, then it was that the apostles as a group became *men of the Spirit*, and as such, the foundation of the Church for all time. This was the birthday of the Christian Church. This is when and how it began. There was nothing like *this Pentecost* before. There will never be anything like it again. It stands for ever in a class by itself. We can't make too much of Whitsunday. We can't make too much of Pentecost.

3. *The Spirit in the Church*

And now, thirdly, note how the apostles all had to be gathered together in one place. From this we may gather that the Holy Spirit is God's gift first of all *to the Church* and not to individuals. Or to express the matter more exactly it is in the Christian fellowship, the believing community, waiting on God, that this experience comes. Perhaps I ought to add 'normally comes' for the Spirit is sovereign, he will act as he will. But where the Spirit is there we may be sure the Church of the risen Christ exists.

Does all this sound too grand, too abstract? Let me tell you of a very ordinary occasion to illustrate the point I am making. Some months ago a friend drove me in her car to a church service, a

Eucharist in which I was taking part, conducted in a language not our own though I had a working knowledge of it. What struck her was the warmth of the fellowship and the welcome which in spite of the language barrier could be felt. Clearly in this place the Spirit of Christ was alive. She recognized it. I recognized it. And in recognizing that distinctive spirit in the fellowhsip, conveyed by the Spirit of God, we knew that this was indeed the Church of God in that place.

No, I am not saying spiritual experience is sufficient to mark out the Church. There have to be preaching and teaching, baptism and the Eucharist, all characteristic of the fellowship as Acts, chapter 2 with its story of the coming of the Spirit goes on to describe, but, without the Spirit of God at work, they are nothing.

4. *God in experience*

Lastly then let me repeat my question—What then is the Holy Spirit? The apostles discovered when they were all together in one place. They knew then that the Holy Spirit is God in our experience. That is to say, the divine was not now to be *out there*, seen, touched and handled, least of all did they receive a theology of the Spirit; there was no explanation of how there could be a Third Person of the Trinity; no, there was an experience of the living God coming upon them, and it had a profound effect at once on their powers as witnesses to the risen Christ. They felt it, they knew it and it was obvious to all who encountered them.

This is possible for us in the Church. We too are able to experience the living God now—his grace, his love, his power, his forgiveness *because* of the Holy Spirit. He is the interpreter of God to us, the communicator, the revealer, the One by whom we can hear God addressing us today, and through whom we can address God in prayer always. It is by the Holy Spirit that Jesus is not only the Jesus of history, the man who walked about in Galilee and Judaea two thousand years ago but *the Christ* of experience now, making an impact on us in the twentieth century. The Holy Spirit makes the Church's ministry possible and your witness and my witness too. There would only be a minimum result from preaching and teaching, however eloquent the speaker, without the co-operating presence of the Holy Spirit, little from the breaking of the bread and the outpouring of the wine in the Holy Communion without that Spirit, and virtually no

3

communion *with God*. It would be an empty rite. So in baptism. The Holy Spirit is God *at work*, it is the power, the transforming power of God in action. Do not try to define the Spirit more precisely. And do not, when we speak of the Person of the Holy Spirit, think in terms of person as we are persons, but only that God acts in a personal way. He is not a machine. A machine doesn't care, it simply functions. And we can only pray to God if he is understood as personal.

What a day then Pentecost is for the whole Christian Church! God is real to us because of it, indeed we live as Christians because of it. The Holy Spirit, as the Creed says, is the Lord and giver of life because through the Spirit we experience the living God now.

2

NEW LIFE THROUGH
THE SPIRIT

*Moreover if the Spirit of him who raised Jesus from the dead
dwells within you, then the God who raised Christ Jesus from the
dead will also give new life to your mortal bodies through his
indwelling Spirit.* Romans 8.11 (NEB)

About eight months ago a call was made in the House of Commons
for the Church of England to be disestablished. A member alleged
that there would be widespread support for this up and down the
country. Such a call is not new; indeed, it is almost perennial. Some
leading figures in the Church of England itself have advocated it. The
tie, they say, represents privilege, bad for both Church and State.

1. *Stabilizing religion*

Disestablishment has not, however, happened; nor does it appear
likely in the foreseeable future. One of the reasons is because religion
is seen as 'the cement of society'. It holds the nation together, acting
like a series of half-invisible tie rods in a great building, for lack of
which the structure would be in danger of falling apart. Moreover,
religion as a stabilizing force is the way in which it has been assessed
down the ages; indeed only in modern times has the idea of a
completely secular state officially separate from religion been advocated and attempted at all.

There is truth in the idea of religion as 'the cement of society'. If
there is no consensus of what constitutes moral behaviour in the
community there is nothing to which to appeal. Even the law is
hampered, and without law there is no order, and without order
chaos reigns. There is fear of such falling apart today; so whatever the
problems associated with an established church, don't take out the
tie rods now; this is the argument. And, after all, in the Bible we see
religion and the state closely intertwined. The Old Testament sets

5

out the association in detail, so much so that a secular state with a disestablished temple is nowhere in sight.

Yet, for all that, there are dangers in state religion—which is why some call for disestablishment of the Church of England today. One danger is conformity, for conformity can take the heart out of religion turning it into little more than respectable behaviour. And people can profess to belong to an established church with no better motive than to receive recognition from authority.

2. *Energizing religion*

Pentecost however breaks in with a different conception of religion altogether. It is everywhere in the New Testament and not without foreshadowing in the Old. Pentecost does not see religion as a conserving force but as an energizing force. It does not seek primarily to stabilize what is, but to break out into new forms of activity altogether. Pentecost is thrusting, inventive, and pulsating with life. Of course there are dangers in it; dangers of excess, lack of balance, and emotionalism, but there is no Christian religion after the pattern of the New Testament in which Pentecost finds no place at all.

Take the day of Pentecost itself as the disciples of Christ are reported in the Acts of the Apostles as having experienced it. They were waiting in expectancy for something to happen, and it did—a spiritual experience so powerful and so consuming that it could only be likened to wind and fire, neither of them stabilizing forces! And the immediate outcome was such a zeal to communicate the gospel of the Risen Christ, and such a success in actually doing it, that even hearers way out beyond their own racial and cultural *milieu* understood. Crowds gathered from all over the city to listen, overtaken with amazement at the enthusiasm they witnessed, such enthusiasm that the scoffers (there are always scoffers) said they must be drunk. And the thrust did not slacken. The Spirit-filled members of the new-born Church crossed old frontiers, broke into new territories, healed sick that appeared incurable, dramatically increased their adherents and incurred the opposition that showed they were alive, because no one bothers with a dead church.

The story of Jesus as set out by St Mark follows the same pattern. Jesus was endowed with the Spirit at the River Jordan and immediately was thrust out into the desert to be tested; and when he had won through, immediately he was out and about in Galilee preaching, calling for discipleship, and healing the lame, the halt and the blind. The pace of his mission was enormous, till of course his opponents closed in and engineered his crucifixion.

Does any of this present the Christian religion as *essentially* a stabilizing force in society, a preserver of the *status quo*, a moral code of decent behaviour? Not that the Christian religion repudiates the need to stabilize society. God forbid. Pentecost, however, tells us that there is far more to our Christian religion than that, and without the spiritual experience, it proclaims, any church is dead, including the established church.

3. *New life*

So what we are thinking about is new life, not simply the maintenance of the old life, but new life developing on the basis of and *out of* the old. It is the Spirit of God which brings this about, the same Spirit as raised Jesus from the grave on Easter Day. We even have a resurrection now, a resurrection destined to be completed on the other side of our death. All this, and more, is implicit in the text chosen for this Pentecost sermon—'Moreover if the Spirit of him who raised Jesus from the dead dwells within you, then the God who raised Jesus from the dead will also give new life to your mortal bodies through his indwelling Spirit.'

But how does one receive this indwelling Spirit? How does the church experience this spiritual Pentecost? By being open to the Risen Christ whom we meet in Jesus of Nazareth, the babe of Bethlehem, the man of Galilee, the preacher, the healer, the crucified Christ. When we acknowledge him, and trust him as the Lord of life, and associate with others who trust him, being open and not closed in heart and mind to him when ministered in Word and Sacrament, then we *catch his Spirit* and are vitalized spiritually. This is our Pentecost. And when this happens we are different, and the whole church is different. It is different even when it is established. The world sees it to be different. They sense a different spirit from that which operates in the world. It is not only kind, caring and generous; it is thrusting, inventive and pulsating with life. No ecclesiastical planning or settlement is a substitute for Pentecost. Pentecost must come first.

7

3

INSPIRED LEADERSHIP

And they were all filled with the Holy Spirit and began to talk in other tongues, as the Spirit gave them power of utterance.
Acts 2.4 (NEB)

For a long time last year we were wondering who was going to succeed Ronald Reagan as President of the United States of America, now we know—Vice-President Bush. In another key, however, the speculation continues. What sort of President will he be? He presents a good image and has wide experience. But is he perhaps a little dull and lacking in sparkle? Could he in any sense be styled a charismatic leader?

1. *Inspired natural leaders*

The word 'charismatic' has become popular these days. Strictly speaking it is a New Testament word referring to a gift of the Spirit, but it has come to mean in popular use anyone who has 'something extra' about his personality, a peculiar power inexplicable solely by his credentials, qualifications or experience. When a charismatic speaker rises to his feet we all listen. Everything about the man is compelling. And if he has wisdom, a sharp intellect and a strong physique as well, crowds are bound to follow him. We call such a man a natural leader.

I wonder if all the twelve apostles were natural leaders? I wonder if this is why Jesus chose them in the first place? Peter certainly was a natural leader. He was always putting himself forward. And James and John, we read, either came themselves, or worked on their mother to approach Jesus and ask for chief places in God's coming Kingdom. The other apostles did not take kindly to their cheek. And Matthew, described in St Matthew's gospel as a tax-gatherer, must have been a pushing type. And then there was Simon the Zealot, obviously a man with strong convictions and ready to act on them. Thomas of course was diffident but not when he was sure of his ground. Philip a bit slow, but not afraid to speak up. Yes, I think all these men were natural leaders. They were all different, but (as we say) they all 'had something'. So Jesus, who could read people, picked them out, and they came to be known simply as 'The Twelve'. Then he spent months, possibly two or three years, teaching them, and that by the most effective method. They lived with him, listened to him and watched him. The best teacher is the model of what he is seeking to teach. So a bond is formed between teacher and taught, essential if the teaching is to be effective and lasting.

In the light of all this, you might have thought, and I might have thought, that nothing else was required for these natural leaders instructed by Christ himself to provide the leadership the newly-to-be founded Church required. They had everything. But had they? Not in the estimate of Jesus who chose them and taught them. They lacked the inspiration of the Spirit and until they experienced this they were to do nothing, except to wait for it to happen. And of course it did, at Pentecost. Then they were all over the place proclaiming the new-found gospel of Christ crucified and risen. No one could stop them. And before many a year was out even Rome itself had to reckon with Christianity.

Surely now the truth stares us in the face. The Church would never have got started, never have grown, never will grow—note that—never will grow—without *inspired*, not simply natural, leaders—however well-educated. The Church must have leaders inspired by the Holy Spirit, and if that is what charismatics are, so be it.

I am not boasting, I have nothing of which to boast. But I began my ministry after ordination as a theological tutor, and have never been completely out of practical touch with teaching students preparing for ordination. I have seen a few with high academic qualifications achieve very little in the pastoral office and almost bore their congregations to tears. I have seen others who must be classed as mediocre by their examination results who nevertheless come to exercise influential ministries evoking the comment, 'I never thought he had it in him!' And I have also seen a tiny handful of others brilliant in academic and natural abilities powerfully inspired by a strong spiritual experience win people left, right and centre for

9

the Kingdom of God—powerful men. How do you explain it? Only one answer is possible. The Holy Spirit had touched their lives. They had become *inspired*, yes, inspired, natural leaders. They had had their Pentecost.

2. *Inspired utterance*

And now let us return to that first Pentecost and see the apostles after their personalities had been quickened by the Holy Spirit. At once they became lively. And when a person is lively, conversation flows. Never again would these men sit glum with nothing to say. Listen to my text again, Acts 2.4: 'And they were all filled with the Holy Spirit and began to talk in other tongues, as the Spirit gave them power of utterance.' No, the meaning is not that they suddenly possessed 'the gift of the gab'. This is not something able to be imparted, not to an East Anglian like me for instance! What happened at Pentecost was that these apostles henceforward displayed an undying urge to declare their faith in Christ, some powerfully like Peter, others no doubt less dramatically but no less convincingly. And this is the point to grasp, those who heard them felt goaded to ask, 'How is it that we hear them, each of us in his own native language?' And the answer must be, Because when these people speak they touch people's hearts, no matter what their racial, social or economic background. These twelve apostles may not have been intellectually brilliant, I do not think they were, and I guess they all spoke with a Galilean accent, but they touched the springs of action in everyone to whom they proclaimed their faith. In listening to these men you forgot these men and knew only that you were being addressed by the living God. This is what the Holy Spirit does.

I am tempted to dodge these 'other tongues' with which the apostles were gifted on the day of Pentecost, because I have to confess I don't know what they were. Were they ecstatic utterances using no known vocabulary, that is 'the speaking in tongues' in which modern Pentecostalists express their ecstatic praying and about which St Paul wrote to the Corinthians who were fascinated by it? Or was there imparted to the apostles an unusual facility to express themselves in current foreign languages so that they could pursue the Christian mission? Such a sudden fluency is not unknown. I am sure however that we shall be wise to leave these questions aside and concentrate instead on *what* the apostles preached so that all who heard them felt compelled to listen, and even change their lives.

Let me tell you a story. A Norwegian soldier called Lars Olsen Skrefsrud (1840–1910) became so drunk and disorderly that even the military prisons refused to detain him. Before, however, he was ejected this ruffian became converted through reading the New Testament in the prison. So powerful was his experience that he determined to become a missionary upon release, but not surprisingly no missionary society would accept the responsibility of a man with such a background. So he went himself to India, and in the course of time founded what became known as the Santal mission. The work was so successful that funds poured in from Europe and America when he travelled there to tell the story. He in fact became famous, so famous that the King of Norway felt bound to invite him to his castle to thank him on behalf of the Norwegian people. At once however Skrefsrud sensed the danger of being himself in the footlights and not the gospel. So when the King enquired how he came to be the master of over forty languages and dialects he replied, 'Your Majesty, it is not important how many languages one can master, but that one has something to say in whatever language one speaks'.

No, do not worry about what these other tongues were with which the apostles spoke so vividly on the day of Pentecost, ask instead *what* it was they preached, for this is where the power lies. They preached Jesus Christ crucified and risen in whom we are offered forgiveness and life eternal.

3. *Varieties of gifts*

And now a *third point* about Pentecost. We ought not to think that the Holy Spirit comes upon Christian people to make us all into preachers. There is not only one gift of the Spirit, namely impressive utterance. To make this clear let me quote from a letter St Paul wrote to the Christians in Corinth (1 Corinthians 12). 'There are varieties of gifts but the same Spirit. There are varieties of service, but the same Lord. There are many forms of work, but all of them, in all men, are the work of the same God. In each of us the Spirit is manifested in one particular way, for some useful purpose.' And in his letter to the Christians in Rome (Romans 12), 'The gifts we possess differ as they are allotted to us by God's grace, and must be exercised accordingly:

11

the gift of inspired utterance, for example, in proportion to a man's faith; or the gift of administration, in administration. A teacher should employ his gift in teaching, and one who has the gift of stirring speech should use it to stir his hearers.'

So on the day of Pentecost the apostles were not all made into first-class preachers. I can't, for instance, think that Philip ever became such, but maybe a gifted administrator. And Thomas a superb teacher. We do not know how each of the apostles was gifted, though it looks as if Peter was the preacher *par excellence*, judging from Acts 2.14ff. But this we can know. The gift which each possessed by *nature* was quickened into striking activity by the coming of the Holy Spirit. Let us be clear on this point. Charismatic or spiritual gifts are not *super*-natural, they are natural but are quickened and made to blossom by the Spirit.

See how far all this is from the kind of power sometimes displayed on the worldly scene. There have been, there are, people who work as if possessed; something seems to have come over them; they may even be said to possess a demon. The apostles bore no resemblance to this, nor is 'possession' any part of distinctive Christian experience. Those upon whom the Spirit descends remain themselves. They do not wait for anything to 'come over' them. Instead they are made aware of the gift they possess, and do not hide it like the third man in the parable Jesus told, but use it in the service of others. In doing so they become twice, three times, four times (how shall we measure it?) what they were before.

Come back then to the first Pentecost. Please do not write it off as 'airy-fairy' suitable only to rarefied and mystical types of people. It is down to earth and practical, perhaps more than any part of the whole Christian experience. Here the apostles became superbly equipped men, men to be reckoned with, men the Church could not do without; all different from each other but all together in their common belief in the Risen Lord. The Church was built on such men and can never do without them. Yes, we must have Pentecost, we must have the Pentecost experience today.

4

THE SECOND PENTECOST

*Peter was still speaking when the Holy Spirit came upon all who
were listening to the message.* Acts 10.44 (NEB)

It would be a reasonable guess that all Church people know about
Whitsunday, at least they will have heard of it; and perhaps a great
many other people, too, who would not count themselves Church
people. After all it used to be a Bank Holiday. We remember what
produces a holiday! What is more we may even be acquainted with a
few details—the apostles gathered together in Jerusalem; and suddenly the sound as of a rushing mighty wind; and the Spirit of God
descending as it were tongues of fire; and how the recipients in a
new-found life and enthusiasm 'began to speak in other tongues as
the Spirit gave them utterance'. So wrote St Luke in chapter 2 of the
Acts of the Apostles.

Yes, maybe we know this, but who knows that there was a second
day of Pentecost? This also St Luke described, this time in chapters
10 and 11 of the same book, writing it out at length to make it
memorable. But the difference is that on this occasion those on
whom the Spirit descended were not Jews, they were not apostles,
nor did the event take place in the holy city of Jerusalem, but in the
Roman garrison town of Caesarea down on the Mediterranean coast,
where a centurion, a Roman army major, had assembled his relatives
and friends, everyone of them a Gentile, that is a non-Jew, to hear St
Peter deliver the Christian message. Listen to the text again—'Peter
was still speaking when the Holy Spirit came upon all who were
listening to the message.'

1. *God has no favourites*

We take this lying down but not if we have even an inkling of the
loathing with which the Jews at that time looked on all Gentiles.

13

They wouldn't sit down to a meal with them. They wouldn't even cross the threshold of their houses. And they included the Romans, masters of the known world though they were, and enjoying living standards that surprise us even today when we uncover them through archaeological research. Nevertheless as a people the Romans could be, and very often were, disgustingly brutal, coarse and cruelly grasping. But there must have been exceptions, and Cornelius, a centurion or major in that section of the Roman army called the Italian Cohort, stationed in Caesarea, must have been one of them.

We must never condemn whole peoples in the lump. God doesn't. Somehow or other some people manage to live godly lives in a godless environment. Was that great French writer, Emile Zola, in his novel *L'Assommoir* making this point in his long and sordid description of the slums of Paris at the turn of the century where the only relief seemed to be in drunkenness or prostitution,—was he making this point when he drew a picture of the girl Lalie living an exemplary life of self-sacrifice? She almost strains our credulity, but so does Cornelius! Did this tough Roman commander really gather together his relatives and friends in the garrison town of Caesarea to hear St Peter, a Jew by race, present the message of Jesus? St Luke's account in chapters 10 and 11 takes some believing but we must believe it. This thing happened, and there is something even more startling to come than the opening words in St Peter's sermon 'I now see how true it is that God has no favourites, but that in every nation the man who is godfearing and does what is right is acceptable to him'!

2. *To whom God the Holy Spirit comes*

And now let us hear the text again. 'Peter was still speaking when the Holy Spirit came upon all who were listening to the message.' So straight away we can rub out race as the qualifying factor as to who shall, and who shall not, be endowed with God the Holy Spirit. St Luke, in his account at Acts 10.45, allows no one to be mistaken over this. He wrote 'The believers who had come with Peter, men of Jewish birth, were astonished that the gift of the Holy Spirit should have been poured out even on Gentiles. For they could hear them speaking in tongues of ecstasy and acclaiming the greatness of God.' And of course we can rub out gender as the qualifying factor, for the

14

relations of Cornelius wouldn't all be males! No, the Spirit of God will come to all and any who are willing to say 'yes' to the message of Jesus Christ.

And what is that message? What was it on Peter's lips? We are left in no doubt. It was all about historical events, not about feelings, aspirations or even conduct. It centred entirely on Jesus Christ; 'how God anointed him with the Holy Spirit and with power'; how 'he went about doing good' and how the apostles could bear witness to what he did, and how he was put to death by hanging on a gibbet and how God raised him to life on the third day. This risen Christ commanded the apostles to proclaim to the people him who will one day be judge of the living and the dead. Everyone who trusts in him receives forgiveness of sins through his name.

Was this a 'one-off' sermon that Peter preached to Cornelius, his relations and friends at Caesarea? Certainly not. It was a repetition of the constant theme of all the preaching that the apostles undertook in the early days of the Christian Church. It was almost wholly centred upon Christ, his life, death and resurrection, duly witnessed, on the strength of which God's forgiveness of sins is proclaimed.

Here was preaching not written off as irrelevant. Here was preaching entirely different from mere moral exhortation and certainly different from scolding, though there might have been grounds for such. What is more there was no call for a particular kind of conversion experience. Peter set forth Christ. That is all, but what an 'all' it is. Such preaching is proper Christian preaching. And the result? It took everyone's breath away. Hear our text again: 'Peter was still speaking when the Holy Spirit came upon all who were listening to the message.' You could tell because the congregation came alive with an ecstasy of praise.

So now we know. God the Holy Spirit enters into the lives of all, whoever they may be, who sincerely believe the message of Jesus Christ who lived, died and rose again. The basis is as simple as that!

3. *The organized Church*

And now we must be careful. To get bogged down at this point in theological discussions, be they never so learned, about water baptism, baptism in the Spirit, and whether or not these two always correspond, is to miss the point of the sequel to the event we have

15

been considering. 'Then he (Peter) ordered them to be baptized in the name of Jesus Christ.' Not that I wish to write off the propriety of these questions. Please do not misunderstand me. There is a place for them. But the point here is that the spiritual experience which Cornelius and his company underwent when they responded to Peter's preaching was not to be left as sufficient by itself. It had to be tied into the organized Church by the gate of entry called baptism in the name of Jesus Christ.

It is not uncommon for individuals who have undergone a striking spiritual experience to count this as self-sufficient and to look askance at organized religion, perhaps as it shows itself in the local Church. There is almost a widespread feeling abroad that Christ is acceptable but not organized religion for it is formal if not hypocritical. Unfortunately organized religion is sometimes, perhaps frequently, formal if not a little hypocritical, and some people love to have it so because then it makes few demands on them and seems to offer a plausible ground for neglect. But we cannot in the pride of self-sufficiency over our own spiritual experience cut ourselves off from the organized Church. Note how strong is the wording at Acts 10.48 where the outpouring of the Spirit of God on Cornelius, his relations and friends is described. 'Then he (Peter) ordered them to be baptized in the name of Jesus Christ.'

Do you reckon that Cornelius and his friends were all what we might call 'charismatics' (as popularly understood) after this experience? I do not. Cornelius continued to be a Roman centurion ordering his troops about. But I guess he was different. I guess his fellow soldiers in the barracks at Caesarea remarked on the difference. Not only was he more generous but there was a sense of purpose and meaning in his life they wished they possessed.

No, the coming of the Spirit of God into our lives does not make us all extraordinary in the sense of achievement. We shall not all be gifted in languages overnight, nor enthusiastic evangelists, nor brilliant organizers and teachers, though some undoubtedly will; but we shall all exhibit a little more of the Spirit of Christ in our dealings with other people, and that will be quite remarkable in a selfish, grasping, deceitful world.

I think back to my years in Hampstead. Just at the point where the railway line from Euston to Liverpool and the north-west issues from the tunnel on leaving Euston, there used to be an allotment on the

16

banked-up ground close to the track. From time to time a man could be seen there tending his potatoes, vegetable marrows and carrots. I knew that man. He lived with his wife in a mews flat over the railway wall. He had been a coachman but when coaches were given up he became a chauffeur. I do not know that he possessed any skills beyond growing vegetables and maintaining a car, but as honorary verger at the local church (the war-time congregation was so depleted there was no money to pay him) his kindly smile and general help-fulness as people entered the church was no small part of the reason why they loved the place and continued to come. Clearly that man had received the gift of God the Holy Spirit. I know because St Paul wrote in his letter to the Christians in Galatia 'the harvest of the Spirit is love, joy, peace, patience, kindness, goodness, fidelity, gentleness and self-control'. Yes, if perchance you had looked out of the carriage window as the train issued from the tunnel on leaving Euston and saw a man in an open-necked shirt and corduroy trousers digging over his allotment, you would be seeing a man upon whom the Spirit of God had fallen, though he would be surprised if you told him. He had the Spirit because sometime in his life he had said 'yes' to the message of Jesus Christ; just like Cornelius and his friends at Caesarea when they accepted what Peter preached to them.

Hear the text once more. Acts 10.44: 'Peter was still speaking when the Holy Spirit came upon all who were listening to the message.'

5

THE MAN OF THE SPIRIT

'The Spirit of the Lord is upon me because he has anointed me;
he has sent me to announce good news to the poor,
to proclaim release for prisoners and recovery of sight for the blind;
to let the broken victims go free,
to proclaim the year of the Lord's favour.' Luke 4.18, 19 (NEB)

1. *The carpenter*

When the preacher read out this text from Isaiah in the Nazareth synagogue everyone's eyes were fixed on him. They were fixed on his hands, strong, ingrained workman's hands, not a bit like a professional preacher's hands; but then they knew him, he had worked as a carpenter there in Nazareth. Time and time again they had seen him making his way along the narrow street with perhaps a stout wooden beam on his shoulder for some building construction, or delivering a wooden ploughshare to a neighbour, or entering a house with his bag of tools to repair a piece of furniture. Everyone knew the local carpenter, he was a necessary and respected member of the community. And he wore the badge of his calling, a small chip of wood behind his ear, just as a scribe had a quill pen thrust into his belt, and a dyer a piece of coloured rag. People knew the preacher's father too, also a carpenter, and all the members of the family. Villagers do, and Nazareth was not much more than a village.

So here was the local carpenter up in the local pulpit. But this sermon was not his first. He had toured the whole countryside preaching in the synagogues and won a glowing reputation. No wonder the congregation assembled in the Nazareth synagogue with expectancy, though mixed with a measure of resentment that he had not graced their pulpit before. But when they heard him they were not disappointed. There was a stir of admiration in the place. He surpassed all the professional preachers they could remember.

Except for those hands he did not look like a carpenter. He did not sound like a carpenter. Yet they knew him as Joseph's son. They had known Joseph. It was all very puzzling.

And of course you will know that I am speaking of Jesus the erstwhile carpenter in the Nazareth pulpit; and how contrary were the reactions of the congregation as soon as he opened his mouth. They often are to a sermon. But in the Nazareth synagogue that sabbath the members of the congregation had 'to give it to him' as we say, he was an arresting preacher—that voice, that diction, those eyes, that presence. But they also knew his family, they knew his background, he had been 'a blue collar worker'! What had he to say to them?

2. *The anointed Son of God*

He would have had nothing to say but for the experience that had come to him after he had closed his carpenter's shop door for the last time and quitted Nazareth; nothing, that is, in comparison with his preaching after that event, deep as was his communion with God and his insight into people's hearts and minds. I refer to his baptism in the river Jordan by John which turned out to be his anointing by God with the Holy Spirit. He had no public ministry till this had taken place. It was a turning point in his life.

I shall not be divulging any secrets if I say that for the closing six years of my ministry I occupied a position from which I was able to watch fairly closely a number of clergymen appointed to high office in the Church. I saw what stepping up on to a more public and responsible platform did to these men. It changed them. They gradually became more expansive, more confident, more thrusting. I remembered being warned when I was preparing for ordination myself, years and years ago, not to rely on what the holding of an office gave you but what you brought to the office. There is truth in this, and no doubt there was wisdom in passing on the warning to a young man; but it only represents part of the truth. If a man is chosen for high office, and knows he has been chosen from among others, he will rise to it. The office will change him.

All this is but a pale reflection of what happened to Jesus but it is a reflection. He was a carpenter, no doubt a skilled carpenter and highly respected as such in Nazareth. We need carpenters. His was

19

however a limited life. Few would ever know of him outside his locality. But he was called on to such a public platform that his name came to be on everyone's lips, and because of this fame even on the Roman governor's lips. But the change did not merely happen. That is to say he did not simply slide from being a carpenter into being a preacher, teacher, healer and all the other descriptions we give him. He was chosen, he was appointed, he was equipped at a particular time and place.

This is what happened. Shutting up his carpentry business, he trekked down to the river Jordan there to associate himself with the impressive moral reform movement which was shaking the whole country under the leadership of John the Baptist. Crowds stepped down into the river to be baptized by John, symbolizing repentance. Then, to his confusion, John saw Jesus also stepping down into the water. How embarrassing! Surely for John to be baptized by Jesus would make more sense. But no, Jesus stepped down, right down, he was baptized like everyone else. Then it happened. What happened beggars description. Only symbols will do. I relay them from St Mark's account of Jesus at that moment, 'He saw the heavens torn open and the Spirit, like a dove, descending upon him. And a voice spoke from heaven: "Thou art my Son, my Beloved; on thee my favour rests."'

He was never the same again. He wasn't a carpenter any more. He had become the *Man of the Spirit*. Perhaps no one expressed this more simply than St Peter preaching to Cornelius and his extended family at Caesarea, 'You know about Jesus of Nazareth, how God anointed him with the Holy Spirit and with power. He went about doing good and healing all who were oppressed by the devil, for God was with him' (Acts 10.38 NEB). The Gospels tell the story, and what a story it is! A breathless narrative, especially St Mark's. Jesus reaching out to people everywhere touching with those powerful hands of his, the blind, the lame, the warped, the diseased, even lepers no one would touch, outcasts, men and women in the gutters of society, until of course the authorities jealous of his authority got him and killed him, but even that death came to be felt as the healing touch of God for mankind.

One of the classical paintings which always claims my attention is that by Michelangelo on the ceiling of the Sistine Chapel in Rome. God the creator reaching out to touch with the tip of his finger the tip of the finger of Adam, giving him life. This is how God reached out in Christ to touch those in need whom he encountered. He had been equipped by the Holy Spirit of God at his baptism to do this very thing. Here then we have a picture of what the Holy Spirit at all times is—God reaching out to touch us where we are, healing us with his life.

Go back now to that Nazareth synagogue that Sabbath day when all the people sat there agog with the ex-carpenter up in the pulpit. No, don't look at those strong hands now. Don't ask questions about his family. Listen to what he is saying.

'The Spirit of the Lord is upon me because he has anointed me;
he has sent me to announce good news to the poor,
to proclaim release for prisoners and recovery of sight for the blind;
to let the broken victims go free,
to proclaim the year of the Lord's favour.'

The Holy Spirit is the hand of God, the finger of God, reaching out in Christ, and through those who own his name, to succour, heal and even sometimes to refrain. The Holy Spirit is God at work.

3. *Men and women of the Spirit*

And now a question. Why was Jesus the ex-carpenter anointed with the Holy Spirit at his baptism in the river Jordan? The quick answer is—so as to equip him with God's power for his tremendous ministry. It was God's power that was working such wonders in Judaea and Galilee. It was not the carpenter's power. Jesus claimed nothing for himself. With great emphasis Jesus is reported by St John saying, 'In truth, in very truth I tell you, the Son can do nothing by himself' (John 5.19). Not that he was a mere cipher. His manhood was real, very real, but because he did not ground his ministry in any exceptional powers of his own, humbling himself as the ex-carpenter to be baptized with sinners like everyone else, he was appointed to be *the Man of the Spirit* and show forth *God's power*. And not only to show forth God's power but to make his Spirit, the Spirit of Christ, dwell and operate in those who believe in him. This is the significance of Pentecost.

Let me end with a story. It comes from America. A woman was in a hospital lift on the way to visit a friend who was making a good recovery. On the way up, the lift stopped to admit a nurse and a young man cringing in pain. 'Take us straight up to the operating floor' said the nurse to the lift attendant. As he did so the boy turned an agonized face on the visiting woman and gasped 'Lady, can you pray? I'm scared. This has all happened so fast.' Surprised at her own calm, she grasped his outstretched hands and prayed 'Our heavenly Father, come close to this boy. Be with him; give him courage; take away his fear. Stay with him constantly, through Jesus Christ our Lord.' The lift stopped at the top floor. 'You pray now' she said to the boy. But he shook his head. 'Say a little prayer then which your mother taught you.' The lift attendant made no move to open the doors. The boy did pray. It was very simple. Then the doors slid back and the nurse helped him painfully towards the operating room. Next day the lady was visiting her friend again. All at once she was aware of the nurse she had met in the lift. 'How is the boy?' she asked. 'You know' replied the nurse, 'we are not supposed to say what goes on in hospitals but I have special permission this time. Just before the boy went under the anaesthetic he said, "Please tell the lady in the lift that I am not scared now, and I think I feel God close to me".'

'O, how wonderful' came the quick response. 'How is he? When can I see him?' To which she replied, 'Everything was done for him but he died under the operation'.

No, not even when we live and work in the Spirit of Christ as this woman obviously did, be it in lifts, hospitals or anywhere else, can we count on miracles. But we shall be reaching out to people where they are, as she reached out. It is the ministry to which all Christians are called and not only called but equipped, for Jesus received the Spirit at his baptism so that we might receive the power of the same Spirit through our faith in him. We shall even surprise ourselves with what we can do, and more important still—actually be.

6

THE LIBERATING SPIRIT

Where the Spirit of the Lord is, there is liberty.
2 Corinthians 3.17

There is no living condition more sought after today, or ever has been, or more prized, and yet more tantalizing, than the one I am about to try and handle now. I refer to liberty. Everyone wants liberty. Everyone wants to be free. Freedom is the great 'in word' of the twentieth century fuelled by the aspirations which surfaced in the nineteenth. And if we aren't talking about how to acquire freedom—freedom of speech, freedom of information, freedom from want, freedom from fear, freedom from nuclear weapons, freedom from pollution—we are talking about how to safeguard our freedoms. Tankfuls of ink have been emptied in writing about freedom, some of the writing inflammatory, some of it philosophical and hard to understand. What can I hope to accomplish in one sermon? Perhaps I am foolish to make the attempt! Yet this text from St Paul's second letter to the Corinthians stares me in the face, 'Where the Spirit of the Lord is, there is liberty'. What shall I say?

1. *The secret of a happy community*

First, that *the spirit* in a community, not compulsive rules, is the secret of a happy community and a successful community because it allows for liberty.

Here are two identical families living opposite each other. Father, mother, two teenage boys and a younger girl. Each family is 'comfortably off'—small car, annual holiday abroad, television, wall-to-wall carpet. The family on one side of the road is constantly split with rows. In the summer when windows are open you can hear the strident voices as the members of the family 'go for each other'. And then the front door is slammed and someone strides out in high

23

dudgeon. Clearly there is rebellion in that household. No one is going to do what is asked, and the more that is demanded the more the rebellion.

Now cross the road. On the other side are the same external circumstances but no rows. Disagreements, yes, sometimes; disappointments and occasionally individual members of the family have to put up with what they do not like. But there is no walking out, no deliberate taunting or giving of offence. And the more remarkable contrast from the house opposite is that there do not seem to be any rules and regulations. But the family is a happy one, and a successful one. Why? because there is a *good spirit* in that family and a lack of it across the way.

So the spirit is that which makes for a happy, successful and peaceful community because it allows for liberty and is not repressive. So my text for today, 'Where the Spirit of the Lord is, there is liberty'.

Is it beside the point, then, to comment that in our country today, deeply disturbed as it is by vandalism, violence, drug addiction and fraud, is it beside the point to say that stricter rules and regulations, however necessary in the short term, are not the final answer? Rules enforced inflame because they infringe liberty, and infringed liberty inflames rebellion. There has to be a new spirit abroad, and I have to confess that I do not know how this is to be brought about except by the birth of Christian faith in the hearts of people. Surely it is to this the Churches should be bending all their energies. 'Where the Spirit of the Lord is, there is liberty' and a much higher standard of happiness and achievement as a result. Evangelism should be the priority now.

2. *Spiritual not legal religion*

And something else. When the principle embodied in this text, 'Where the Spirit of the Lord is, there is liberty', is neglected in church life, religion shows up as a cramping, burdensome thing. From being a liberating experience of the Spirit, it has degenerated into a repressive system of rules and regulations. This, unfortunately, is ever the tendency in every branch of the Church. Where this hardening takes over the Catholic becomes enslaved to the minutiae of correct ritual, the Protestant to strict Reformation

24

doctrine, and the Evangelical sects to a standardized mode of Christian experience. And then the dynamism is lost, and what is left is routine religion or mere moralism, unattractive to the outsider. Nor is this the whole of the tragedy. The participants in it tend to be 'little people'.

What a problem even St Paul had with this! He wrote about it in his letter to the Galatian Church using strong language and mightily taking his leaders to task for going back on the religion of the Spirit in which they had begun as Christians. Now they were caught in the bondage of ancient religious customs, taboos and regulations inimical to their life and liberty. Did the Galatians heed his words? Has the Church ever consistently heeded his words? Yes it has, at certain times, though often with long intervals of deafness in between. Then it sparked into life again. Perhaps the present time with the Charismatic Movement is such a time. If so, we should be thankful.

But the Church remains chary. It has seen how the outcome of reliance on the Spirit can be fanaticism and that fanaticism is dangerous. Reliance on the Spirit can also lead to a chaotic life of immorality under the misapprehension that liberty means licence—do as you like. A spiritual religion, however, is in no way indifferent to behaviour. On the contrary what is looked for is a Christ-likeness in action and bearing; and this is the point: Christ-likeness is not achieveable by the imposition of rules and regulations. Only through love and loyalty freely given does this come about. Have we not seen what love of a girl will cause a young man to do for her? And what a girl will do for him? Love is the elevating force in life, not law. Law only damps down and checks. All this is why religion must take to heart this text, 'Where the Spirit of the Lord is, there is liberty'.

imitators of Christ

3. *The spirit of the age*

Is there anything else, any other kind of bondage from which the Spirit releases us? Yes, the spirit (small 's') of the age, what the Germans call the *Zeitgeist*. It is very powerful. It enslaves people. One of the forms in which it manifests itself is fashion, and I do not only refer to clothes but to behaviour patterns. The temptation to do what everyone does is very strong. Young people especially dare not step out of line, though sometimes they find the courage and the individuality.

I was reading the other day of a young man at his first job after training. He thought he ought to attend the firm's social club with his other workmates at the end of the week. He did attend. He attended in his best suit. But he did not like what he saw, his workmates drowning themselves in liquor till they could scarcely stand. But they did not like what they saw either, a young man *not* getting drunk. So one of their number carried over to him a large glass of beer and poured it over that nice new suit . . .

No, swimming against the tide isn't easy, but there are times when it is right to do so and not become a slave to fashion. And the Spirit of the Lord in a man or woman helps them to be free as nothing else can.

4. *Bondage to self*

One last point, and perhaps most important of all, the Spirit of the Lord releases us from imprisonment to self. Nothing dwarfs us, nothing warps us so much as self-centredness, nothing is more difficult from which to find release. We are all caught here, almost from infancy, till we find the way out, and the way is hard.

But 'where the Spirit of the Lord is, there is liberty' from this bondage because the Lord is the Lord Jesus Christ and we know how unselfseeking he was, indeed he gave his life for others. All who have the Spirit of Christ within them progressively get free from selfishness.

I was reading recently, though I can't remember where, about a large residential school for boys mainly of limited means. I think it was in Yorkshire. That I have forgotten all the details and where-abouts is significant because it shows up what caught my attention— the school matron. Apparently generations of school leavers, whatever they had forgotten about their early education did not forget this woman. They used to ask after her and even visit her. Yet she was 'nothing to look at'; unkind people said it was not surprising she was unmarried. But the boys all knew that whatever scrapes they got into, whatever accidents, illness or troubles at home she was always there helping. In fact everyone simply expected her to be there. They took her for granted. Yet she sought nothing for herself and made no demands about her rights, it was to be wondered if she ever took time off. She seemed utterly and completely free from self-centredness; and never strained and never depressing. If ever the Spirit of Christ, God the Holy Spirit, operated in a life, it did so in the case of that school matron. She was no prisoner of self-centredness or selfishness. She was and looked completely free, a shining example of my text, 'Where the Spirit of the Lord is, there is liberty'. Where the Spirit of Christ reigns there is freedom from the self. Lord, give me grace, give us grace to receive it.

7

THE CREATOR SPIRIT

In the beginning of creation, when God made heaven and earth, the earth was without form and void, with darkness over the face of the abyss, and a mighty wind that swept over the surface of the waters.
Genesis 1.1, 2 (NEB)

Ever since Pentecost, Whitsunday, we have been turning our attention to the Holy Spirit in the course of our worship. And we began, as was to be expected, with the story of the descent of the Spirit on the apostles like a powerful wind and flames of fire. So we have been concentrating on the living God *in experience*, the experience of the Church and our experience. What is more, this is where the Bible places almost all its emphasis, God the Holy Spirit in action *for us*.

There is, however, another, and perhaps more fundamental aspect of the Spirit which calls for our attention, it could almost be called the secular awareness of the Spirit, I refer to God the Creator Spirit—*Creator Spiritus*. To consider this is salutary lest we fall into the ever-present trap of cutting down the Spirit to fit our experience, dwarfing what is infinite, and taming it and even accommodating it to our ecclesiastical structures. The Holy Spirit is far and away greater than our experience of him could possibly be. And this is nowhere brought home to us more impressively than in the metaphor the Bible uses of the Spirit of God as wind, strong, powerful and mysterious. For some of us this was imprinted startlingly on our minds on 16 October 1987.

I was up early. Everyone else in the south-east of England was up early. We couldn't stay in bed after first light. We had to see what the wind had done during the night. We did see. I saw. My garden reminded me of nothing so much as the pictures I had been shown as a small boy of the trees and woods on the battlefields of France in the First World War ripped apart and uprooted by shell fire. My garden resembled a battlefield. Huge branches were strewn everywhere. A sturdy lime tree lay across the road. Fir trees leaned at threatening angles. Apple trees lay sadly on their sides. And as the day wore on we learned the full extent of the devastation, there were no trains, no buses, no electricity. The entire landscape looked different. And the cause? Wind, nothing but wind untempered, tearing and terrifying.

1. *God the Holy Spirit as a wind*

The Hebrews of the Old Testament regarded the winds with awe as well they might. Without the winter winds from the sea to the west of their country there would be no rain, and no rain meant no food. Their livelihood, indeed their life depended on that wind and its regularity. But there was also the hot, the scorching wind from the north called the sirocco. When it blew, and it wasn't confined entirely to October, you took cover for it boded no good to life and limb. No wonder the Hebrews took the wind seriously, they had a word for it—*Ruach*—it occurs again and again in the Old Testament.

That the Bible uses this word—*Ruach*—as a metaphor for God the Holy Spirit may surprise us. I put it this way because so many of us, brought up with the hymn by Harriet Auber (1773–1862), never conceived of the Holy Spirit in these forceful terms but rather—

> And his that gentle voice we hear,
> Soft as the breath of even,
> That checks each fault, that calms each fear,
> And speaks of heaven.

And who will deny that on occasions this is true to experience? But *Ruach*, wind, points rather to a disturbing power that is primordial, creative, life-giving and sometimes frightening. You stand in awe of the wind, if indeed you can stand against it at all. And you can't escape it, you have to reckon with it. The wind is one of the given things in the natural order. So is the Holy Spirit of God. This is where we have to begin if ever we are to understand.

2. *God creating*

The Holy Spirit, then, is God creating. This is what he is. We may go further, wherever we see creative work there is the Spirit of God in action. We should see this primarily in the world of nature, its magnificence, its variety, its wealth of material, its beauty. The natural world has not come about by chance, nor is it sustained by chance. The Spirit of God is constantly creating and recreating it. Creation is a continuous process and the Spirit of God is the agent of it.

A few days ago I came across this little story. It was about a school mistress teaching her class about the seven days of creation as set out in the book of Genesis. As expression work she gave each child the task of drawing a picture of one day of creation. You can imagine what fun it was depicting the sun, moon and stars; and of course the fish, birds and animals—and especially man—'male and female created he them'. But what about the seventh day when God rested from all that he had created and made? What could the small boy do who was allocated this? But apparently he found no difficulty at all! He simply drew an empty chair. 'But why empty?' he was asked, for an old and bearded man fast asleep might have been expected. 'Because', replied the boy, 'because when God had finished what he had created and made he did not leave it alone, he was out and about keeping it all going.' He spoke wiser than he knew. The creation is a continuous process, not a once and for all event in the past. And the agent of the process is God the Creator Spirit.

This then is the force that sustains the world of nature. Sometimes even the most pedestrian of us sense this as we gaze in wonder at the beauty of a blood-red sunset, or the intricate loveliness of some tiny flower or the migratory instinct of birds, surely one of the wonders of the world. This is something the poets are able to capture in words and convey to us. It is no small part of their ministry. But may we go further? May we see the divine Creator Spirit in the skilful creative work of *human* hands? The Bible would seem to suggest this for in Exodus 31 we read:

> The Lord spoke to Moses and said, Mark this: I have specially chosen Bezalel son of Uri, son of Hur, of the tribe of Judah. I have filled him with divine spirit, making him skilful and ingenious, expert in every craft, and a master of design, whether in gold, silver, copper, or cutting stones to be set, or carving wood, for workmanship of every kind. Further, I have appointed Aholiab son of Ahisamach of the tribe of Dan to help him, and *I have endowed every skilled craftsman with the skill which he has.* (italics mine)

Sometimes when I have stood in amazement at the intricate stonework of one of our cathedrals, or the exquisite finery of the Crown jewels, or the precision of the tiniest parts of a piece of machinery produced by modern technology, I have had no difficulty in believing this. To look with wonder at all work that is creative is to look at God the Creator Spirit in action. And, as we think of Pentecost and the Spirit coming as the life of the Church and of ordinary people like you and me, this cosmic creative aspect of the Holy Spirit must not be forgotten. We are touching, and being touched here by something tremendous. We do well to stand in awe.

3. The Spirit gives life

And now we take up the telling phrase in the Nicene Creed

> We believe in the Holy Spirit,
> the Lord, the giver of life.

Nowhere is the Holy Spirit as the giver of life given greater prominence than in St Luke's birth narratives of Jesus. I quote; ' "Do not be afraid, Mary, for God has been gracious to you; you shall conceive and bear a son, and you shall give him the name Jesus" . . . "How can this be" said Mary, "when I have no husband?" The angel answered, "*The Holy Spirit* will come upon you, and the power of the Most High will overshadow you . . ." '

Indeed all the events surrounding this birth are linked with the Holy Spirit. The forerunner of Jesus, John, is described as 'filled with the Holy Spirit'. Even John's mother, Elizabeth, greeted by Mary and feeling her baby stir in her womb was so filled with the Holy Spirit as to cry out, 'God's blessing is on you above all women'. And Zechariah, the father, was filled with the Holy Spirit when he uttered what we call the *Benedictus*; and Simeon when he spoke the *Nunc Dimittis*. When life was coming into the world, new life, significant life, and a birth never to be forgotten, the agent of it all was the Holy Spirit of God. This is why we repeat when we assemble for the worship of God in Christ

> We believe in the Holy Spirit,
> the Lord, the giver of life.

What we see then in the opening sentences of the Bible is the Spirit of God depicted as wind—*Ruach*—brooding over the formless void of

31

the abyss and bringing to birth life, life of immense variety, beauty and richness, indeed the fascinating world we know.

And when we turn to the opening description of the Church as set out in the Acts of the Apostles, we see the Spirit of God depicted as a mighty wind bringing life to the twelve apostles making them new men, men on fire to proclaim the message of the living Christ. Here was new life, new birth, the birthday of the Christian Church. At Pentecost it was born from above.

Is this mere history? It certainly is history but it is more; it is a picture of contemporary experience. Whenever and wherever men and women open up to faith in the risen Christ, the Holy Spirit brings them new life, life from above, they are born anew, they are a new creation. Inexplicable? Yes, of course, inexplicable like the wind. It 'blows where it wills, and you hear the sound of it but do not know whence it comes or whither it goes', as Jesus' said to Nicodemus, 'So is it with everyone who is born of the Spirit.'

Never underestimate, then, the power of the Spirit; never pass off the Spirit as a mere name in an ecclesiastical formula. The reference is to the Creator Spirit, the one who brings life into being and order out of chaos. The Hebrews thought of the Spirit as *Ruach*, a strong and mighty wind. We do well to retain this metaphor. Our religious faith will never be narrow and insipid if we do.

8

OUR CORRESPONDING SPIRIT

The Spirit himself beareth witness with our spirit that we are the children of God. Romans 8.16 (RV)

A little time ago I lost my car keys. Perhaps you know how frustrating this experience can be. I searched high and low. I tried to remember what clothes I was wearing when last I drove the car and searched the appropriate pockets. I almost crawled over the garage floor, but to no avail. Last of all I was reduced to borrowing my wife's set of keys and having them copied at the local locksmith's. Then, mine 'turned up' (as we say). They would! How I wished then that I had a device such as a friend of mine has attached to her car keys. When she whistles, the attachment responds with an audible bleep, as much as to say, 'Here I am, you can find me here'.

In our modern world, ever since the invention of sound radio, what we used to call 'the wireless', we have grown accustomed to the principle of a sound made in one place being answered by a corresponding sound in another place, although there is no visible connection. This is because they are tuned in to each other, or to employ the technical jargon, they are 'on the same wavelength'.

1. *The human spirit*

I hope you will not write this off as too crude an illustration but I need something to try and show how God communicates with us and how we, human beings, can communicate with God; and my difficulty is to avoid providing an explanation so theologically or even psychologically abstract as to help no one. So please suffer my illustration about being so made as to be on the wavelength of God. 'The Spirit himself beareth witness with our spirit that we are the children of God.'

There is a common feeling abroad, perhaps there always has been, that religion is all right for those who are 'made that way'. It is conceived of as a kind of idiosyncrasy. This, however, is not so. Everyone has spiritual potential. This is what makes for the human. It differentiates the human from the animal, and of course from a thing. A rough indication of this may perhaps be found in the recent Gallup Poll where as high as eighty per cent of people confessed to a belief in the existence of God, which is not, of course, to say that it is operative to much extent in their lives; but *it is there*. One writer has expressed this by asserting that each one of us consists of body and soul (or mind) and a God-shaped blank waiting to be occupied. This is what I have called 'the spirit', written with a small 's', able to be connected to the divine Spirit written with a capital 'S'. But suppose it never is connected. Suppose the God-shaped blank is left unoccupied, deserted, neglected or even desecrated. Then the person becomes spiritually dead, it shows in the face. So the humanity gets diseased, and in the worst cases, perhaps a minority, the result is evil men. We really do neglect the spiritual in us at our peril, because it is there in all of us. It is what makes humans human.

The upshot of all this is that no one need feel self-conscious about possessing a religious awareness, it is not pathological, it is not abnormal.

2. *Call and response*

Come back now to my illustration of being on the same wavelength making call and response possible. I can whistle for my car keys if I have lost them and there will be a corresponding whistle on the receiver attached to the keys indicating their whereabouts. But I do have to whistle, and the receiver attached to the keys does have to respond. So in spite of the theological and psychological truth that there is in everyone of us a spiritual receiver corresponding to the Spirit of God it does have to be put into service, it does have to respond to the address of the divine Spirit.

At some time or other, in the course of our lives, and in some way or other, each of us experiences that address, perhaps vaguely, perhaps sharply. It may be through the impact of a scene of exquisite natural beauty, or some moving piece of music, or the mystery of falling in love. Then we sense a dimension other than the human and material, and play with the idea of the divine and spiritual. Or more pointedly conscience stirs us—something we have done or left undone. More disturbingly the fact of Christ will not go away. It is like a telephone bell, perhaps in another room which we can just hear. It is waiting to be answered. 'What do you think of Christ?' It stops. Later it rings again. Many people take the receiver off. Some do not.

The classical case of answering the disturbing fact of Christ is that of Paul, or more accurately Saul of Tarsus. I hesitate to refer to it because it has the demerit of being dramatic and so may be dismissed as having no relevance for us. Most of us do not experience anything in such lurid colours. I certainly have not. Saul, nevertheless, did hear the insistent call, 'Saul, Saul, why do you persecute me?' I have no doubt he heard that ringing again and again long before he answered it on that momentous day when he was taking the road to Damascus in order to imprison yet more Christians, torturing them to confess, for he counted them heretics and enemies of Israel. But I do not think he was converted there and then on the road. I think he was beaten down. I think he was in darkness not only physically, having been blinded by what happened on the road, but spiritually. So he was led into Damascus. And there after three days' misery, through the ministry of one called Ananias he responded in his spirit to the call of the divine Spirit and became a different man. Listen to the way St Luke put it. 'Saul, my brother, the Lord Jesus who appeared to you on your way here has sent me so that you may recover your sight, and be filled with the Holy Spirit'. Note when the Spirit descends, immediately the call is answered.

No, a dramatic conversion experience is not an intrinsic part of the gospel, and those high-powered evangelistic campaigns which seem to make it so are mistaken. The gospel, the good news, is Christ crucified and risen for us offering us the forgiveness of sins and the promise of eternal life. But when the Spirit brings this gospel home to our spirit, maybe dramatically, maybe undramatically, *we must respond*; otherwise the human spirit is left like an empty house liable to be spoiled. But when we do respond we become inwardly convinced that we are the children of God. Listen to the text again, 'The Spirit himself beareth witness with our spirit that we are the children of God' (Romans 8.16).

3. *Children of God*

I like the phrase 'children of God' which the Spirit communicates to our spirits when we respond to his call. We are not called 'men of God'. There was only one Man of God and his name was Jesus. A child is a small creature, dependent, easily hurt and often puzzled and yet eager. Sometimes the child is naughty, answers back and refuses correction. We are *children* of God. I myself would not wish to claim any more superior spiritual stature than this, and if ever any one of us should be tempted to feel more, a reminder of what we are is salutary; children of God, not more, not less.

Children however have a father, and God is like a good father to us his children. He cares and he provides. So we are not waifs and strays in the world with nowhere to go. Our standing, though humble, is secure. And children play. Mostly they enjoy life because they are cared for, they laugh and are merry. If only all of us who are the children of God could appear a bit more like the children we really are, how much more attractive would we be, and the gospel we seek to proclaim.

Do not be taken up then wholly with *the manner* of God's communication with us, that is the divine Spirit to our human spirits; grasp *the content* of the message—we are the children of God. What a privilege! What a source of inner peace and joy.

'The Spirit himself beareth witness with our spirit that we are the children of God' (Romans 8.16).

9

THREE STAGES IN RELATIONSHIP

To prove that you are sons, God has sent into our hearts the Spirit
of his Son, crying 'Abba!, Father!' You are therefore no longer a
slave but a son, and if a son, then also by God's own act an heir.
Galatians 4.6, 7 (NEB)

On 5 October 1988 there appeared in the newspaper a brief report
about a 'live-in' nurse in Hampshire, aged forty-four, who had been
looking after a retired ship-broker, eighty years old, a widower with no
children. After five months he died and in his will left her rather more
than half a million pounds which was not contested by any relative. Of
course our first reaction is to raise our eyebrows in astonishment,
accompanied no doubt by a variety of ejaculatory remarks each characteristic of the individual uttering them. But what about the nurse?
How did she react? This is not the aspect on which I wish to comment,
much less speculate; rather to note the three stages in relationship to
the deceased through which she must have passed. First she was a paid
servant, no more, no less. Then, secondly, she must have been treated
like a daughter, an adopted daughter. And then, thirdly, she became
his heir—servant, adopted child, heir. This progression, I submit, on
the basis of Galatians 4.7, is open to us in our relationship to God
through the action of God the Holy Spirit. Listen to the text again, 'To
prove that you are sons, God has sent into our hearts the Spirit of his
Son, crying "Abba! Father!" You are therefore no longer a slave but a
son, and if a son, then also by God's own act an heir.'

1. *A slave of God*

Three successive stages in our relationship to God then—slave, son,
heir. First slave. The Greek word here is *doulos*. It was a common
word in that old Roman world in which the Church grew up. There
were thousands upon thousands of slaves, mostly foreigners, mostly

prisoners-of-war; in fact in Rome itself the number of slaves so outnumbered their masters that revolt by them was a perpetual threat. And when in 73 BC they did rebel, led by Spartacus, the consul Crassus had six thousand of them crucified by the side of the Appian Way that led to Rome. But not all the slaves were harshly treated, some of them were much better educated than their Roman masters, especially those captured in Greece, a few even came to be adopted. History gives some striking examples. Nevertheless a slave was a slave, someone without rights let alone privileges, kept only for the work he, she was able to perform.

In the light of this, then, how could we ever be classed as the slaves of God? God is not a taskmaster. God is not a tyrant. God cracks no whips over us to make us work faster, submit more meekly, suffer more brutally for our various wrong doings. No, but is not that precisely how thousands upon thousands of people look upon God? Is this not why they try to propitiate him, keep him quiet, and compensate for their misdeeds? They reckon God is out to crack down on us at any moment, that is to say, they have made for themselves a *slave-like mentality*, they have even become slaves, slaves of God; hence the lucky charms, the amulets and all the rest of the paraphernalia which even sophisticated men and women can be found wearing designed to stave off the sudden swoops of a capricious God. And what shall we say of the modern slavery to the false gods of money, sex and power?

There needs to be a war against slavery of the mind in the contemporary world, and what the New Testament proclaims is that God the Holy Spirit possesses the power to pursue it. So my text again—'To prove that you are sons, God has sent into our hearts the Spirit of his Son, crying "Abba! Father!" You are therefore no longer a slave but a son, and if a son, then also by God's own act an heir.'

2. *A son of God*

A second stage in our relationship to God is that of being a son. Not that any one of us could ever call himself the Son of God, capital 'S'— there was only one such, Jesus of Nazareth—but we can count ourselves as sons of God, small 's', or more precisely as *adopted* sons of God, privileged to call God 'Our Father who art in heaven' with all the advantages son-ship involves in contrast to the status of being a servant or a slave.

I don't want, however, for a moment to give the impression that so to conceive of God is easy. There are grown men and women, let alone children, for whom the word 'father' carries a repelling overtone. If ever you have read the book *Father and Son* first published anonymously in 1907 by Sir Edmund Gosse, as he became, librarian of the House of Lords, telling of his overbearing narrowly religious father and what he in consequence suffered, you will know what I mean. And to be the son of a famous father can be crippling to a sensitive adolescent. And fathers can be over-indulgent, especially to daughters, ultimately ruining their happiness; a picture painted in startling colours by Galsworthy in his classic novel sequence, *The Forsyte Saga*, in the characters of Soames and Fleur. No, the metaphor 'Father' for God is not obviously serviceable. What has to be in mind is a good father in a good family circle, one who is firm as well as loving, caring and close. When you see or hear of such a father you sit up and take notice as I did when I read the appreciation of the late Geoffrey Lampe, sometime Regius Professor of Divinity at Cambridge, not from academics, these I expected, but from his daughter testifying to what a wonderful father he had been, and how much she owed in her life to what he gave her of himself.

I submit to you that so to think of God is not easy, and consciousness of it at all times does not come readily to most of us. We tend to half conceive of God as far off and not a little demanding. And if we reckon that the New Testament, or even the teaching of Jesus, takes it for granted that we shall count God as Our Father, I fear we have got it all wrong. It takes a great deal out of us to see God in this fashion. What is more, it takes a great deal out of God! He had to *show* he cared for us, had to show he was prepared to come close to us, had to show that we counted in his sight. But all this he has done in the life, death and resurrection of Jesus Christ. This is what the New Testament is all about. And when we grasp it, when we believe this of God, then his Spirit evokes the answering signal in our spirits in the confidence of which we dare to whisper 'Our Father who art in heaven', or as they said it in Aramaic, the language Jesus used, 'Abba! Father!'

What difference does this confession make? I'll tell you, tell you from my own experience, albeit with diffidence. It takes the fear of life away, anyway some of it, I wish I could say more, but I have still so much to learn and practise. God being our Father does not mean that he changes our circumstances for us. We shall still have to go on living in the same old world, full of traps, troubles and traumas; but God is with us in it, alongside of us even, as our Father. That is the difference this testimony of the Holy Spirit in our heart makes. Then we hear God's word spoken through many pages of the Bible, 'Do not be afraid', and we shall not be, not quite so much anyway.

3. *An heir*

And now I am 'up against it' to find an illustration for this third stage in relationship—being made an heir. I have never been an heir to a fortune, though various public enterprises seem anxious to try and convince me that several thousands of pounds await me round the corner if only I will fill in this coupon, hazard a guess about that diagram, or buy some special product. I suppose one of the primary effects of finding oneself heir to a fortune is the feeling that somehow with all that money the future is now assured, except of course that it cannot stave off the incidence of illness or accident.

All this at least casts one light on our text, it looks forward to the future, to the future beyond our present life here on earth. Not only are we through faith in the risen Christ and the power of his Spirit lifted out of the status of being servants into the privilege of being sons of God so that we can call on God as our Father and so our fears are countered, we are promised glory in the life beyond. Much as we have received of joy and gladness in the here and now, through our faith, there is more to come, infinitely more in heaven. We are made heirs of all this and the Spirit of God witnessing in our spirits is the foretaste; or as Ephesians 1.14 expresses it, 'that Spirit is the pledge that we shall enter upon our heritage, when God has redeemed what is his own, to his praise and glory'.

So then let us lift up our hearts with joy and our heads with confidence. We are no longer trapped in the slave mentality of God as a tyrant; instead we are privileged to walk as sons of God even though maybe at times shakily, and, what is more, we have an assured future beyond the grave. Hear our text again, Galatians 4.6 and 7: 'To prove that you are sons, God has sent into our hearts the Spirit of his Son, crying "Abba! Father!" You are therefore no longer a slave but a son, and if a son, then also by God's own act an heir.'

10

THE HARVEST OF THE SPIRIT

But the harvest of the Spirit is love, joy, peace, patience, kindness, goodness, fidelity, gentleness, and self-control.
Galatians 5.22, 23 (NEB)

When I announced that after Pentecost I would preach about the Holy Spirit I guessed that some might decide there and then that the subject was not for them. It was too 'way out', even liable, possibly, to cause personal eccentricity; or if not that, it was a subject for high-powered Christians, missionaries perhaps, or preachers, or leaders of evangelistic movements, but not for engineers, housewives, schoolteachers, hairdressers, computer technicians and the like. You would not be likely to find yourself on an underground train or a bus talking to a man or woman in whom the Holy Spirit dwelt, or so you would think. Such a person, you would reckon, would be bound to look distinctly odd.

1. *The Spirit in everyday living*

But are you correct to think like this? We have been, or we shall be giving our attention to the *gifts* of the Spirit and some, indeed, are extra-ordinary, that is outside the ordinary; but so are some of the gifts of nature. Let the point be made strong and clear, the gifts of the Spirit are not supernatural gifts, they do not drop down from heaven, they are natural gifts quickened or enlivened by the Spirit. I am not, however, asking about these at the moment, I am asking how the Holy Spirit affects the ordinary day to day living of Christian people. The answer is to be found in St Paul's letter to the Christians in Galatia, chapter 5, verses 22, 23: 'But the harvest of the Spirit is love, joy, peace, patience, kindness, goodness, fidelity, gentleness and self-control.' Nothing very high-powered there surely! No call to be an evangelist in Hyde Park or to organize bumper fundraising

41

campaigns, right and proper as these striking efforts may be for the few who are called to them. No, the harvest of the Spirit is to be looked for first of all in people's disposition. Listen to the list again—'love, joy, peace, patience, kindness, goodness, fidelity, gentleness, and self-control'. The other day I saw the owner of a village corner shop come round from behind his counter where he had been serving a little old lady hobbling with two sticks and help her, not only out of the shop, but across the road. I am sure I was seeing a tiny piece of the harvest of the Spirit.

But what about this list of virtues? If you possess an analytical type of mind you might see how they fall into three groups of three. First a general attitude—love, joy, peace. Secondly an attitude to people—patience, kindness, goodness. Thirdly the principles that govern behaviour in general—fidelity, gentleness, self-control. I can't imagine there were many people walking about in Galatia displaying the totality of these virtues any more than in London, Leeds or Littlehampton; but they do describe the ideal Christian life. This is the pattern anyone in the following of Christ should set before him, and to provide the incentive and power to approach it is the work of the Holy Spirit.

I don't know if the New English Bible is strictly correct in translating St Paul's word *karpos* in this verse as 'harvest'. 'But the *harvest* of the Spirit is love, joy, peace' etc., but I like it because so often the verse is misquoted as 'But the fruits (plural) of the Spirit . . .'. This is not what St Paul wrote. It is not possible to separate out these virtues as if they were apples on a tree and we could boast, 'Well I have one anyway, perhaps two, of these virtues, and two out of nine isn't bad!' No, all these virtues merge into each other and produce *the general character* of the life that is influenced by the Holy Spirit. And this we must note—love comes first. Without love, love of God, love of his children, all his children, black, white, yellow, working people (so-called), professionals, yuppies, clever people, clumsy people, men and women you don't particularly like, even enemies (there is the rub), without love we shall not sustain the virtues we possess. Put this way we shall have to concede that in default of the Holy Spirit, no one of us will ever come near reaching this standard of spiritual excellence. But then no one ever has, except Christ, which is why we need his Spirit, the Holy Spirit, to put us in the way of it.

2. Love, joy, peace

(a) Now let us look at the first trio of virtues. It begins with love. I have to confess I do not find this easy to visualize. I once heard the late Archbishop Fisher call it a 'slippery word', meaning, I suppose, that it represents different ideas to different people—a powerful emotion that hits you like falling in love, or admiration, or sentimentality, or a mere preference ('I love smoked salmon'), or sexual intercourse. We are in a real difficulty here. Perhaps the word 'love' has been so bandied about that it has become practically useless to describe the basis of the Christian character or 'harvest of the Spirit'. Perhaps we shall have to 'make do' with a summary statement like 'doing unto others what you would like them to do to you'. Try this out on someone you find peculiarly difficult or who doesn't attract you. I think you will discover you need some of the other virtues also in St Paul's list such as patience, kindness and self-control. Love really is a comprehensive virtue as well as a basic one.

(b) And now joy. 'The harvest of the Spirit is joy.' In Acts, chapter 8 we read that when Philip went down to Samaria and preached the good news of Christ there was much joy in that city. I am sure there was because Philip was a man 'full of faith and of the Holy Spirit'. Wherever there is a response to true Christian preaching, joy is one of the observable outcomes. But were these Samaritans all jolly in consequence? Perhaps they did all clap hands, dance around and sing choruses. I don't know. I am ignorant of the Samaritan temperament. But of this I am quite certain: Christians are ill-advised that to show themselves as Spirit-led they must appear jolly. This is artificial. Life has its jolly times—thank God; but it is not jolly all the time. And Christian worship is badly served if so conducted as to appear as if it were. There must be plaintive tunes in our singing as well as triumphant ones, hesitancy in face of life's mysteries as well as strong assurance of salvation. The Psalms can be our guide. They contain Hallelujahs but also crying and tears. And suppose a man with a broken heart creeps in to a church seeking for something, he scarcely knows what—this does happen, I have been a preacher in a central London church and I know—and he is confronted with jollity and a slap on the shoulder, he will not come again. His sensibilities will have been sorely wounded. I repeat, Christian joy is not jollity, it is more like serenity, product of the conviction that God will see us

43

through the dark stretches of life. Therefore the face of the man or woman in whom is the Spirit of God is not slow to break into a smile. All will be well in the end.

(c) And now peace. 'The harvest of the Spirit is . . . peace'. There will not be peace where there is no love. You can tell by noting that the opposite of love is hate and hate makes for war. One in whom the Spirit of God dwells, because he/she cares about people, does not pick quarrels, does not enjoy a row, does not 'take it out' on all and sundry if 'things go wrong' for him. He makes for peace. He quietens people down. He quietens himself down. Of a person in whom the Spirit of God dwells it could never be said, 'When he/she is around the sparks fly'. On the contrary his/her very presence eases the tension in a situation. Love and therefore peace is at work.

3. *A harvest by responding*

'The harvest of the Spirit is love, joy, peace.' Yes, but we cannot work up any of these virtues. It is not possible to make yourself loving, nor to make yourself joyful. I cannot conceive of any sight more pathetic than a person trying to be joyful. Perhaps it is possible actively to bring about easing tension between persons and if the result is not exactly peace, it is better than hostility. The truth is these distinctively Christian virtues are the outcome of response not effort, response that is to the love of God shown in Christ. God cares for you. He cares for me astonishing as this may sound, and at times very hard to grasp. If however we do respond, if we do relax into the love of God there is a harvest the products of which are love, joy, peace, patience, kindness, goodness, fidelity, gentleness and self-control. Overnight? No! no harvest appears overnight. Time is required before any harvest is apparent, and not every harvest is a bumper one. There may even be a poor harvest one year, but harvests there will be, 'seed time and harvest will not cease'. Our wisdom then is to keep hold of the love of God by all the means of grace open to us—Bible reading, Holy Communion, private prayer, the Christian fellowship and the friendship of committed Christian men and women. Then there will be a harvest of the Spirit. There is bound to be. What is more we shall enjoy it. Harvests are always times for thanksgiving, yes, even for jollity. Why not?

44

11

INDIVIDUAL GIFTS OF
THE SPIRIT

*In each of us the Spirit is manifested in one particular way, for some
useful purpose.* 1 Corinthians 12.7

When I was making my way to my car last Whitsunday through the
churchyard of the village church where I had been celebrating the
Eucharist a member of the congregation caught up with me because, as
she put it, she wished to ask me something. I wondered what was
coming. Then she put a straight question, 'Do you speak with
tongues?' Immediately I was on my guard. Speaking with tongues is a
controversial subject but no good would come, I knew, by evasion. So I
replied, 'No, I do not, I lack that particular gift; but I know that some
people possess it, and in the Pentecostal Movement it has indi-
cated a remarkable vitality of spiritual life.' Having said that, did I
wait with some apprehension about her reaction to my confession of
this lack? I think I did, because I recall how a few years back in my
congregation in London a young woman having apparently profited
by the ministry there over a period of many months finally 'gave me
up' (I think sadly) because she felt she had to face what to her was a
regrettable fact—I had not been 'baptized in the Spirit ' . . . So would
I be written off again? But the lady replied, 'We do not all have the
same gifts; we have different gifts for different ministries. You are a
teacher. Not all can teach. Not all can speak in tongues.' And when I
asked if she spoke in tongues she replied, 'Not in public, but in private
prayer sometimes yes'. By that time I had reached my car by the
lychgate and she hers. We parted with understanding, well contented.

I can imagine that to some good people, probably very many, this
all sounds like 'double Dutch'. What is all this about speaking with
tongues, spiritual gifts and baptism in the Spirit? Isn't it all a bit
'cranky', even fanatical, and therefore dangerous? Yes, it could be,
and sometimes unfortunately is, but, it is a serious subject to which
considerable attention is given in the New Testament not least with
the object of encouraging a balanced view of it.

45

1. *A variety of gifts*

First of all, it needs to be said, loud and clear, that each one of us has a gift, a natural gift, a gift of nature peculiar to himself/herself. You remember the parable of the talents which Jesus told? Each of the master's three servants was given an initial endowment of money with which to trade, one five talents, another two, another one. And in the parable of the pounds each of the nobleman's ten servants received a pound, with which to make more. Yes, we all have received some gift. None of us is completely unendowed. But this is not all. When we open our hearts and minds to Christ, and the Spirit of Christ, who is the Holy Spirit, those gifts are enriched, sometimes mightily, the increase in no way diminishing the variety.

I understood this more clearly when I came across (in Bittlinger's book *Gnadengaben*: 1966, ET *Gifts and Graces*) an illustration used by Cyril of Jerusalem (AD 315–386); 'Why did Christ name the grace of the Spirit water? Water is contained in everything; plants and animals need water for their life; in the form of rain, water comes from heaven. It comes down in that one form, but it then works in many different ways. One and the same spring irrigates the garden, and one and the same rain falls on the whole world. But then it becomes white in the lily, red in the rose, dark yellow in the daffodil and hyacinth. In every variety of colour it appears in such different kinds of things. It takes one form in the palm tree, quite another in the vine. In each it is different, although in itself it is always the same. The rain itself never changes and comes down, now in one way, now in another, but it still aims to become the essence of the thing which receives it, and becomes whatever is appropriate to that. So it is with the Holy Spirit, who is one only and undivided but yet gives himself to each as He will.'

One point needs to be added. The gifts of nature and the gifts of the Spirit are not imparted for the self-satisfaction or self-aggrandizement of the recipients but for the service of others. Hear the text again from 1 Corinthians 12.7. 'In each of us the Spirit is manifested in one particular way, *for some useful purpose.*' If spiritual gifts are misappropriated they may do positive harm to the recipients and to the community in which they are exercised. This was the trouble in Corinth and the problem St Paul had to combat there. The Corinthians as a people loved spectacular and showy performances whether of a secular or religious kind. So they 'fell for' such gifts of the Spirit as prophesying, speaking with tongues and healing, passing by very often the spiritual graces such as love, joy, peace, longsuffering and so on. In 1 Corinthians, chapter 12, therefore, straight speaking on the spiritual gifts is to be found culminating in the famous 'more excellent way' of chapter 13 to which I shall come in a minute.

2. *Speaking in tongues and healing*

First a comment on two spiritual gifts which are found to be puzzling by many people. One is speaking with tongues. It is primarily associated with prayer. There is prayer *with the mind* which most of us can readily recognize. In our worship, especially mainstream Anglican worship, this is how we pray. And in our private prayers we do likewise. But there is also prayer *with the spirit*. In this he or she is so charged emotionally that the lips move and sounds are uttered which are not recognizable words. Something like this is recorded in 1 Samuel 1.12–15, 'And it came to pass, as she continued praying before the Lord, that Eli marked her mouth. Now Hannah, she spake in her heart; only her lips moved, but her voice was not heard: therefore Eli thought she had been drunken. And Eli said unto her, How long wilt thou be drunken? put away thy wine from thee. And Hannah answered and said, No, my lord, I am a woman of a sorrowful spirit: I have drunk neither wine nor strong drink, but have poured out my soul before the Lord.' You will remember that, according to Acts 2.13, the apostles on the day of Pentecost when filled with the Holy Spirit and speaking with other tongues were charged by the mocking outsiders with being drunk. Granted that speaking with tongues may seem strange to us, especially to East Anglians like myself who are by nature reserved and unemotional; nevertheless we ought not to write it off as mere gibberish, and certainly not as possession by some kind of external spiritual force. We should recognize it as prayer so fervent that it cannot be contained by conventional language. Is it to this that St Paul refers in Romans 8.26 when writing 'We do not even know how we ought to pray, but through our *inarticulate groans* the Spirit himself is pleading for us'? Whether or not such praying in the course of public worship is to be encouraged is a matter over which even St Paul was doubtful. See 1 Corinthians 14.28.

And now the gift of healing: this refers primarily to the healing of physical illness but also to the restoration of wholeness to the body, mind and spirit. No one prepared to accept the New Testament can dispute that Jesus was a healer and that the apostles administered bodily healing. Nor that healings without the aid of surgery or medicines do occur today. Very many cases are reported and to be sceptical about them all cannot be reasonable. Surely the truth is that some people do possess the gift of healing, yes by nature; and when this is quickened by the Spirit indwelling in the healer it is potent indeed and *a sign* of God's presence. The cases of healing reported in the gospels were such signs, the power to heal however is always a gift, there is no way of obtaining it unless it happens to be given and there is no technique or expertise by which it can be made to work. Nor do we know who may be healed, and who not, though apparently there is such a gift as 'a spirit of discernment'. There is no case in the New Testament of any sick person brought to Jesus who was not healed but some sufferers outside the gospel records had to continue with their infirmity as did St Paul himself. What all this means is that the gift of healing is indeed a reality and the Church is wise to take the ministry of healing seriously. Yet none of this carries the corollary that the normal practice of medicine can be disregarded as of a lower order. The doctor and the nurse in the intensive care unit working prayerfully as well as scientifically are as much exercising the Spirit's power as the so-called 'faith healer'.

3. *The more excellent way*

Have I pitched all this in a low key? I have done so purposely. When St Paul had almost come to the end of his great chapter (1 Corinthians 12) concerning spiritual gifts he wrote this—and I quote from the Authorized Version changing one word—love instead of charity—

> Have all the gifts of healing? do all speak with tongues? do all interpret? But covet earnestly the best gifts; and yet I show unto you *a more excellent way*. Though I speak with the tongues of men and of angels, and have not love I am become as sounding brass or a tinkling cymbal. Love suffereth long, and is kind; love envieth not, love vaunteth not itself, is not puffed up ... Love never faileth: but whether there be prophesies, they shall fail, whether

there be tongues they shall cease, whether there be knowledge, it shall vanish away. For we know in part, and we prophesy in part, but when that which is perfect is come, then that which is in part shall be done away ... And now abideth faith, hope, love, but the greatest of these is love.

So spiritual gifts have only a limited life. There is no eternity in them. They exist for some useful purpose in the here and now and are not to be exercised for selfish ends though that is the danger of them. Love however lasts for ever. It lasts into the eternal world which indeed is its origin. Love moreover is the way by which the other gifts profit those who possess them and those on whose behalf they are exercised. 'Love never faileth.'

It has been my good fortune to know a number of Christian women of outstanding gifts, some indeed quite striking. And I have admired them and been fascinated by them, and learned from them many valuable lessons. But they have not all been caring people. They have not all been people to whom I would instinctively turn in trouble, certainly not if my heart were broken. They have been accomplished and efficient but cold. It is in the light of this that I understand 1 Corinthians 13 telling of the way which is more excellent than the seeking of spiritual gifts. Fortunately this excellent way is within the grasp of the very humblest of us all. Limited as many of us are—I speak for myself—we can put self last and care for others. Then we shall really be demonstrators of the Holy Spirit at work, for there is the Spirit of Christ, and we know how he cared, how he loved.

12

THE SPIRIT PRAYS
FOR US

*In the same way the Spirit comes to the aid of our weakness. We do
not even know how we ought to pray, but through our inarticulate
groans the Spirit himself is pleading for us, and God who searches
our inmost being knows what the Spirit means, because he pleads
for God's people in God's own way.*   Romans 8.26, 27 (NEB)

Out of the many stories about the late Archbishop Ramsey I like this
one. Someone asked him how long he spent in prayer each morning.
'About one minute' he replied. And then noting the shock from the
Archbishop confessing that he only spent so short a time in prayer,
he added, 'but it takes me twenty-nine minutes to get there'.

1. *God's presence*

What lies behind this is an understanding of prayer very different
from that which many of us entertain. Prayer is not primarily—I said
primarily—asking God for things or even for things for other people,
it is being *in God's presence*, indeed at its deepest and most real level it
is in *the consciousness* of being there. Apparently the experience did
not come easily to Archbishop Ramsey but the one minute in God's
presence was more of the reality of prayer than all the twenty-nine
minutes of preparation or approach.

To come into God's presence never is easy. For a start to be still
isn't easy. The mind swims with the activities of the coming day, full
of plans, full of the comments we would like to make to the people we
shall meet, full perhaps of anxieties. Try as we may, these externals
come crowding in to our minds as soon as we attempt to be still. The
truth is it is not easy to dump this baggage on the threshold of God's
presence and be still, even for one minute. Nevertheless that is the
place—still in God's presence—where prayer is prayer.

Perhaps the best analogy of prayer is human friendship with

another person. What we seek most of all in friendship is simply to be with that person. We do not rush in with a series of requests. There is no agenda. And the deeper the friendship the less is talking necessary. The friends are simply happy to be together. They cannot always be so for there are other calls on them, not least of work, which may involve periods of separation, but they will retain the longing to be together again and make opportunities for it to happen. And then they will share their thoughts and possibly feelings. Prayer is like that. It is being in God's presence. And the trouble to arrive there is counted worthwhile. We read in Luke 6.12 that Jesus climbed a mountain to be alone with God, and he continued all night in prayer. We are not to imagine he was asking God for things all the night long; no, he was consciously in God's presence, and that he climbed a mountain (or if you prefer, sought the solitude of the hills) in order to be there suggests the effort that is required to accomplish it.

2. *Our Father*

But what should be in our minds when we are still in God's presence? What should be our attitude? How should we comport ourselves? After all we are on earth and God is in heaven. We are created beings and he is the Creator. We are mortals and he is immortal. Jesus tells us. The dominant thought in our minds must be '*Our Father!*' Our Father reminds us of the care and compassion of God for us, but it also reminds us of his transcendence—Our Father *who art in heaven*. We must bear in mind his Otherness, his Majesty, his Holiness. So, 'Our Father who art in heaven *hallowed be* thy name'.

Part of the preparation for prayer, then, is to think where we are coming, and be conscious of our unworthiness to come at all, but also to be thankful that the way to God is open to us through Christ.

And then we make our requests, the Lord's Prayer encourages this—'Give us this day our daily bread'; but we make these requests conscious of the necessity for God's will to be supreme not our own, 'Thy will be done'. Indeed no small part of the purpose of prayer is to bring our wills into line with his will so far as we can perceive it. All this conditions the way in which we present our requests. We cannot tell God what he should do. We need not give him information about our needs or other people's needs. The proper way in prayer is simply to mention those needs and the people we care about *in God's presence*, or to use an old-fashioned phrase, to lay our burdens at Jesus's feet and leave them there. After all we do not always, if ever, know what is best, but God knows.

Our prayers will always be fumbling exercises even if we doll them up in the cadences of Elizabethan English. Sometimes they will be little more than a recital of complaints (O yes, see the Psalms), and a recital of other people's woes. St Paul knew all about this inadequacy of our praying which is why he wrote in the words of my text, 'We do not even know how we ought to pray', but then we are not on our own in our praying, for 'the Spirit comes to the aid of our weakness. Through our inarticulate groans (what a way to describe prayer!) the Spirit himself is pleading for us', in fact 'we have an Advocate with the Father' who so presents our feeble attempts at prayer that God will hear and answer. Do we need confirmation of this? Then we have the words of Jesus as the fourth gospel presents them the night before his death, 'And I will ask the Father and he will give you another to be your Advocate who will be with you for ever, the Spirit of truth' (John 14.16, 17 NEB).

3. *Corporate prayer*

We have been thinking about private prayer, but there is also corporate prayer, prayer in and with the Church, and in a way this is primary. We read in Acts 2 that following the day of Pentecost those in whom the Spirit dwelt met continually in prayer together. And when we pray on our own we should not forget that we are praying with the Church because we are members of it. It is in the Church, that is in the fellowship of God's people, that his presence is particularly realized. Jesus said 'where two or three have met together in my name, I am there among them' (Matthew 18.20 NEB).

This real and royal presence of God comes to expression powerfully in the Eucharist; which being the case it seems most appropriate that our private prayers for others and for ourselves should find a place there. Ought there not to be therefore space or spaces in Eucharistic worship for silence to make this possible? Every moment ought not to be filled with movement, music and singing. By all means let the service be impressive for we are coming into the presence of the Lord who is King but let there be stillness so that we may feel ourselves there. 'Be still and know that I am God' (Psalm 46.10).

> Speak Lord in the stillness
> While I wait on thee,
> Hushed my heart to listen
> In expectancy.
>
> (E. M. Grimes)

True as all this is we are not to imagine that we can forecast when God will become a real presence in our own experience. After he was risen, Christ did indeed make himself known to two disciples at the end of the road to Emmaus in the breaking of bread, but Mary Magdalene encountered him in a garden, and the disciples gathered together in a room, and seven of them by the lakeside in Galilee when they had been unsuccessfully fishing. We never quite know when. The Spirit of God does not operate according to strict schedules. In a way he is actually untidy. His freedom is as real as that. So I did not blink an eyelid when a lady told me the other day rather reticently (I liked the reticence) that she had recently felt the reality of God as she was sitting alone under a tree in her garden. After all there is the story of Nathanael in John, chapter 1. And some of us know the disturbing reality of the Divine Presence when some passage of the Bible we are reading suddenly 'comes alive'. All at once Truth seems to be standing opposite to us. And then, of course, prayer is the only possible reaction.

What shall we call this? Spiritual experience? And are those who know it for themselves spiritually-minded men and women? And is all this experience to be included under the word 'spirituality'? Of this we can be certain—the Holy Spirit is at work wherever and whenever we find ourselves in the presence of God, it is the Spirit who has brought it about, meeting our spirits (with whom he has affinity) with his quickening and illuminating presence.

Does all this seem way beyond our spiritual capability? We know ourselves to be earthborn creatures, earthy, and immersed in the world's affairs. Most of us are not mystical by nature. But there is good news in my text from Romans 8.26, 27. 'In the same way the Spirit comes to the aid of our weakness. We do not even know how we ought to pray, but through our inarticulate groans the Spirit himself is pleading for us, and God who searches our inmost being knows what the Spirit means, because he pleads for God's people in God's own way.' What a relief! So those sometimes tedious and halting petitions in Church are not wasted effort, nor those feeble prayerful aspirations in the privacy of our hearts. The Spirit presents them in a way that God hears. So let us pray.

13

THE SPIRIT INSPIRES HUMANITY

Then he grasped him by the right hand and pulled him up.
Acts 3.7 (NEB)

The other day I went to buy some support canes for my tomato plants. The assistant who served me (I knew) had worked in that shop for many years. When she took me out to the yard at the back where the canes were stored I asked after the widowed wife of the former owner of the shop now in a nursing home totally paralysed by a stroke—a cabbage-like existence. When I made my enquiry the assistant's eyes softened. For the moment she forgot about my canes. Her mind was on that stricken patient. 'It seems awful', she said, 'to think of her just lying there. She was always so kind to everyone. She was kind to me.' And then, after a pause she added, 'The atmosphere in the shop has never been quite the same since she ceased to be about the place'. As I carried my bamboo canes to my car I thought about the difference one person can make in a community where tensions can so easily arise. The way words are spoken, the offer of a helping hand, the consistently cheerful spirit—so simple, but these are the healing agencies whenever people have to live together. Their worth is enormous.

When we read the story of the first Pentecost in the second chapter of the book of the Acts of the Apostles—the apostles waiting to be clothed with power from on high; and then the sound as of a rushing mighty wind, and cloven tongues like as of fire resting on the heads of each one of them—we expect the results to be astonishing. And they were. The apostles 'began to speak in other tongues as the Spirit gave them utterance'; and so animated was the whole company that unbelieving observers mockingly asserted that they must have been drinking. And then Peter stood up and boldly proclaimed the crucified and risen Christ to the crowds, indeed so convincingly that they cried out for direction how to respond. And what next? The

55

converts to the faith, now rapidly increasing in numbers, regularly met to hear the apostles teach, to share in the common life, to break bread and to pray.

In a way this doesn't surprise us. We half expect the dynamic of the Spirit to be operative, if anywhere, in such ecclesiastical activities as preaching, the Eucharist, and the life of the Church. We construct theologies about the Spirit's operation there. But turn over the page in the Acts of the Apostles and the scene is strikingly different. Nothing typically ecclesiastical here. Instead a man lying on the Temple steps with hand outstretched, begging. He can't walk. He never has walked. Someone dumped him there every morning and collected him every evening. This was all the life he knew. And because he had occupied that site so long most people failed to see him, certainly as a human being, he was just a thing, part of the floor space. Two passers-by however were the exception. They saw him. They saw him differently for they were alive with the Holy Spirit. The name of the one was Peter and the other John. Peter looked at the beggar intently. Was he copying Jesus, his Master, in doing so? Jesus was noted for the way he looked at people.

1. *Seeing*

I suggest the story points up three ways in which we ordinary people can be known to be influenced by the Holy Spirit and the first is the way we see people.

Peter saw this cripple. He saw behind the outstretched hand, the begging bowl, the placard 'Crippled from birth' and the expectant eyes appealing for money. He saw a human being, a human being in which not even the daily dumping on the Temple steps had crushed all hope of something better, not least to be taken for a man, perhaps (God knows) even to be loved a little by someone, a woman perhaps, ugly legs and all. When Peter animated by the Holy Spirit looked at this wretch on the Temple steps, he saw not a deformed beggar but a man. This is what the Holy Spirit in our hearts can do for us—make us see people properly.

Ours is a terrible world for labelling everyone. A man, a woman is working-class, no more, no less. Or a professional, a Socialist, a Tory, a black, an OAP, a yuppie, a vegetarian, a divorcee. And there we stop. But all these people are human beings with hopes and fears and loves and hates. And sometimes they are kept awake at night wondering: Does life have to be so empty as it so often seems to be? And doesn't the crematorium at the end make a mockery of it all anyway?

I want to suggest to you that if the Holy Spirit, the Spirit of Christ has a place within us we shall see people as people. And if we cannot forget the labels altogether, we should never allow them to have the final dismissive word. Everyone is a human being, everyone is a soul, everyone has something absolutely (and I mean absolutely) distinctive about him or her. There are no two persons exactly alike.

I read a short article in the newspaper a few days ago by a diversity of writers who had all taken up painting as a hobby. One of them commented that if painting does nothing else it 'cleans the eyes'. I know this is true. I 'have had a go' at watercolour painting myself, not worth showing the results to anybody, but I know my eyes have been cleaned. In trying to paint I see the countryside as I have never seen it before. I think the Holy Spirit does this for Christian believers. Their eyes are cleansed. They see people and situations in a new way, perhaps for the first time. This is how it was with Peter on the Temple steps shortly after Pentecost.

2. *Speaking*

And now something else from the story of the cripple on the Temple steps. Peter spoke to him. You can be very certain few passers-by did so, not even those who tossed him a coin. You remember of course that when the Holy Spirit descended on the apostles on the Day of Pentecost 'they all began to speak with other tongues as the Spirit gave them utterance'. We think of this in terms of other languages whether rightly or wrongly I don't know. What is clear is they were endowed with powerful, compelling, persuasive speech.

But could we not also read this in a lower key? These Spirit-of-Christ-filled men began to speak in a way other than how people so frequently speak, namely, harshly, rudely, sarcastically, cruelly. Listen to the debates in the House of Commons. Speech may be used as a weapon, an offensive weapon. It may be employed not to enlighten but to confuse. Of Talleyrand, French ambassador to London in 1830–34, it was said that he used words not to reveal his meaning but to conceal it.

None of this is a Christian way of speaking, clever as it may sound. Nor should any Christian count anyone as not worth talking to; no, not even if he is a cripple begging for money on the Temple steps. This is the lesson Peter's action drives home to us. But do we not, all of us, fall into the trap of counting the assistants who serve us in shops and offices as mere functionaries? How often have we a kindly word for them? how rarely even a smile? And the bigger the city, the bigger the business, the less humanity is evident. Believe it or not, there was actually a book written by a theologian not so very long ago justifying treatment of those who serve us in public as parts of the machinery of the enterprise they serve. Peter saw the cripple as a human being and spoke to him. The speaking made Peter human and the cripple human, and all because the Holy Spirit was at work in that situation. Peter spoke, not to gain but to give. 'I have no silver or gold', he said, 'but what I have *I give to you.*'

When I was a young man I used to hear about the Tongues Movement, and now in connection with the Charismatic Revival in the Christian Church I read about speaking with tongues. This is not a gift of the Spirit which has been imparted to me and so any comment of mine on it would lack distinctive value. I could wish however that all Christians would always speak 'with other tongues' than those which are all too common. When people have the Holy Spirit in their lives they do not bite, blaspheme, bicker or bark. There is a proper Christian use of the tongue and it does not include gossip, slander or evil speaking. I will go so far as to assert that you can tell whether anyone is a Spirit-filled Christian by the way they employ words. No Christian can sit lightly to words; they are creative instruments. Was not Jesus called the Word made flesh?

Peter spoke to this helpless cripple tied to one place on the Temple steps by useless legs. It was the experience of the Holy Spirit that made him do it.

3. *Helping*

Thirdly Peter filled with the Holy Spirit grasped the cripple 'by the right hand and pulled him up; and at once his feet and ankles grew strong; he sprang up, stood on his feet, and started to walk'. Is this another action Peter had seen his Master perform? Did not Jesus enter into the room where Peter's mother-in-law lay fever-stricken and take her by the hand and lift her up? And did he not also enter the death chamber of Jairus's twelve-year-old daughter, take hold of her hand and say *Talitha cum*, 'Get up, my child' and immediately she got up and walked about? I warm to this picture. When the child came round from the sleep of death, no doubt bewildered and afraid, the first she knew was that her hand was in the hand of Jesus. Was she afraid any more? Need I ask?

In the light of all this can we not affirm that he/she in whom the Spirit of Christ, the Holy Spirit dwells, is always ready to lend a helping hand to those who are down? They may be people caught in the poverty trap. They may be people caught in the success trap or the luxury trap. Do not imagine it is only the poor whose lives are broken. The Spirit of Christ however leads those in whom he dwells to offer a helping hand *whenever* it is needed.

Have I been touching on simple actions and attitudes in this sermon on the Holy Spirit? Seeing people, talking to them and offering a helping hand? But we make a mistake if we connect the Divine Spirit *only* with complicated theologies and charismatic accomplishments. The Holy Spirit is behind everything which is human and humanitarian. Peter saw, spoke to and helped to his feet that cripple when everyone else passed him by *because of Pentecost*. People who act in that unusual way are a benediction in any community. It could be you. It could be me. Then what a Pentecost!

14

A MAN FULL OF THE HOLY SPIRIT

They elected Stephen, a man full of faith and of the Holy Spirit.
Acts 6.5 (NEB)

Pity about Stephen. I mean about St Stephen's Day falling on 26 December, Boxing Day. Pity because he tends to be overlooked. Of course it is clear why his day is placed where it is—he was the first Christian martyr, or perhaps I ought to say the first Church martyr because there were the Holy Innocents (as we call them), the children killed at the instigation of King Herod, hoping thus to nip in the bud any possible rival to his power and position in the land. We remember them on 28 December. But who remembers St Stephen on Boxing Day? Who reflects on anything serious on Boxing Day? Let alone on martyrdom! Christmas has become so long anticipated, and the day itself so absorbed with eating and drinking festivities that 26 December is rather like the day after the storm. So, pity about Stephen. He gets forgotten. So I have brought him in at another time altogether, I have connected him with Pentecost because it is impossible to reflect on Stephen as the New Testament presents him apart from the Holy Spirit.

1. *An administrator*

Stephen's life in the Church newly-born, born from above, born at Pentecost was very short. No sooner do we hear of him in the Acts of the Apostles than he is a crumpled form beaten to the ground by murderous Jewish stones hurled furiously at him for undercutting racial and spiritual privilege, and charging the nation with resisting the Holy Spirit. But he is no insignificant figure in the story of the growth of the early Church which St Luke has to tell in his book, the Acts of the Apostles. Out of 28 chapters, two whole chapters are devoted to this man. You cannot appreciate the way the Church developed unless you take careful note of Stephen.

60

Stephen, we are told, was filled with the Holy Spirit. This, please note, did not necessarily make him an outstanding figure in accomplishments. We are mistaken if we reckon that the Holy Spirit's function is to double our skills. Stephen was however an outstanding man, he was that by the endowment of nature. He was a born leader. He was one of those men who, wherever you place him, is bound to rise to the top. He had vitality, drive and a sharp intellect. But the Holy Spirit had given him something extra, namely the Christian character, what the New Testament calls 'the fruit of the Spirit'. So he was doubly marked out. When therefore there arose a dispute in the infant Church calling for infinite tact to settle it, and the apostles bade the members search out seven men of good reputation 'full of the Holy Spirit and of wisdom' for this task, all eyes turned first of all to Stephen.

So Stephen became a Church administrator, and ought therefore to be of interest to all ecclesiastical administrators. His job specification was to see that certain women were not discriminated against on racial grounds in the relief fund distribution. So presumably Stephen was concerned with collecting money and allocating it. This would involve conducting enquiries, and no doubt going to see for himself. Every wise administrator does that. And there would also be complaints to investigate and decisions to make, and, I guess, criticisms to put up with. Stephen, however, and the six others with him, 'did a good job' (as we say), the proof being the consequent rapid growth of the Church numerically. Clearly the reputation of the Church, and its gospel, was enhanced by their administration.

Sound administration in a Church is important. It should be entrusted not only to people of good reputation but also 'of the Spirit and of wisdom'. We do well to note the seriousness with which this was taken by the apostles. These administrators after election did not simply slip into their office chairs, they were commissioned by the apostles with the laying-on of hands just like missionaries. There is always however a danger with administration, a double-sided danger; one is that the administrators will be *under*estimated, the other that they will *over*estimate themselves and virtually 'take over'. All too easily the idea gains ground that where the money is there the power lies. This is worldliness, and it is disastrous when it creeps into the Church. The life of the Church is not *produced* by administration though sound administration may help to preserve it. All in all, administration in the Church is only safe when in the hands of spiritually minded men, men like Stephen, of good reputation, of the Holy Spirit and of wisdom.

2. *The preacher*

Yes, Stephen came into prominence as an 'admin' man as we often call such men today, but it was not for his excellence at a desk or for settling disputes that he aroused opposition and finally suffered martyrdom, it was for his inspired utterance. His opponents found 'they could not hold their own against the inspired wisdom with which he spoke' (Acts 6.10). And when they listened to him in the Council chamber, brought there on a trumped-up charge of blasphemy, they couldn't take their eyes off his face.

We ought to note all this. The sharp point of the Church's witness will never be its highly commendable and appropriate social relief work. Similar work will be carried out by people of faiths other than the Christian faith and of no particular religious faith at all. The sharp point of the Church's witness is the gospel which it dares to proclaim. Stephen lay a crumpled corpse battered with stones furiously hurled because, filled with the Holy Spirit, he powerfully preached the crucified and risen Christ who is the Lord we shall face when we die.

Of course we shrink from these religious people who, to quote an old tag, 'are so spiritually-minded they are no earthly good'. Of course we have little time for those men and women so preoccupied with their piety that they have no place in their hearts for the unfortunate, the broken, and certainly none for the weak-willed of this world of whom there are plenty. If, however, the modern Church has nothing else for which to call than better housing, better medical facilities, better pensions and jobs for all, it has no claim to be heard above the other charitable organizations which cover this ground. The Church has to keep its eye on the brutal fragility of human life in spite of, and sometimes because of, our modern technological expertise. The Channel ferry boat disaster, the Armenian earthquake, the Clapham rail crash and the Pan Am plane devastation at Lockerbie are terrible reminders. And not many of us will escape having to line up before the crematorium doors when there is borne in a coffin carrying one who is all the world to us. Yes, we turn away from facing this, but if the Church has nothing much *to say* at times like this, what is the special ground of its existence?

Stephen was praised for his social work in Jerusalem, not to be underrated, but what gave him significance was the gospel he dared to preach, namely Jesus Christ as the Saviour both for now and for eternity. He proclaimed this gospel with wisdom and in the power of the Spirit so that his words became the word of God, the living, goading, breaking and remaking word of God. There was nothing trite about Stephen's preaching, it was decisive preaching, decisive for the hearers, so decisive for some in Jerusalem that they picked up stones to silence him for ever.

Who can read this story about Stephen without seeing that the criterion of the Church's stand is first of all the quality of its preaching—what it has *to say* when life turns rough.

3. *The martyrs*

Stephen has been remembered primarily as the Church's first martyr for the faith. There has come to be a long line of successors to him in this ultimate witness, by no means yet sealed off. Indeed it has been said that more people have suffered for their faith in this twentieth century than in any previous one, most of them without leaving a name or record, indeed known only unto God. Stephen was the first leader of this great multitude. No wonder then the New Testament, economic with its space, devotes six whole verses to describing his death. He was filled with the Holy Spirit when he died, 'and gazing intently up to heaven, saw the glory of God, and Jesus standing at God's right hand. "Look", he said, "there is a rift in the sky; I can see the Son of Man standing at God's right hand!"' It was a testimony which maddened those who heard it even more than his preaching. They 'made one rush at him and, flinging him out of the city, set about stoning him . . . and as they did so, he called out, "Lord Jesus, receive my spirit". Then he fell on his knees and cried aloud, "Lord, do not hold this sin against them", and with that he died.'

Violence and assault are not strangers to us in our cities. We do not have to read this about Stephen to be shocked, we know it all, and worse. We keep this record before us however because it shows us how a Christian died in the power of the Holy Spirit. He passed over the frontier between life and death confident that Christ was waiting there to receive him in the glory of God. And he made the passage with a forgiving spirit towards all who had done him wrong.

Who can read this without hearing the message? We can be confident that when our time comes, please God in a sick bed and not out in the open as the result of violence, we can be confident that God will receive us also in glory; and we should be forgiving to all that have done or wished us harm. This is the way to die. Let Stephen show us, and let the Church continue to tell his story—Stephen the 'admin' man, Stephen the preacher, and Stephen dying confidently in his faith, through the power of the Holy Spirit.

THE SPIRIT NOT FOR PURCHASE

When Simon saw that the Spirit was bestowed through the laying on of the apostles' hands, he offered them money and said, 'Give me the same power too . . .' Acts 8.18 (NEB)

One of the features of the last two decades is the rise of a number of newly-formed religious sects claiming the allegiance of thousands upon thousands of adherents, notably among the 'well-heeled'. There must be money in these movements, or how could they afford the acquisition and maintenance of their prestigious premises?—not least at a time when the established Churches are feeling over-burdened with their existing buildings. Quick-witted people exist however who perceive that it is possible to cash in on religion.

1. *The story of Simon Magus*

That money may be made out of religion is brought to our attention in the New Testament in the course of telling the story of the impressive power of the divine Spirit in the initial building up of the Church. An acute and gifted man called Simon wished to purchase that power, doubtless with an idea of selling it for money. He was popular and made a tremendous name for himself. In the city of Samaria, not only the ordinary people, but the upper levels of society were swept off their feet by his oratory and his works of healing. Clearly this man had power. Some people said the power of God, the 'Great Power'. They acquiesced in the title he assumed—Simon Magus. There was indeed a magic about this man and stories of his activities hung around for more than a century, mostly unreliable, but impressive. And his name is perpetuated in what the law still calls 'simony', that is the illegal practice of obtaining a spiritual or ecclesiastical office by the down payment of money.

So we can't overlook Simon Magus and the unexpected that

happened to him. In Samaria there arrived a far less gifted man than himself who began drawing bigger crowds by his preaching. Worse still Simon's own audience plummeted. It was an experience as bitter as gall. He saw that he possessed a powerful rival. We may guess that he crept in 'at the back' (as we say) to see and hear this rival. Perhaps he wore a disguise lest he be recognized. He ached to discover wherein lay the power of this new preacher. Then what he never dreamed of took place, he found himself hooked by the utterance that riveted him to his seat. Even more, all his resistance was whittled away. He gave in. Gave in to Philip the Evangelist!—for such was his opponent's name. He believed the Gospel of Christ that was proclaimed. At least he thought he believed. Anyway he came forward for baptism and hung on to Philip's presence mesmerized by the powerful signs and miracles he saw taking place. Simon adored power.

2. Simon and his money

I wonder what Philip thought of all this? Was he taken in? Was he taken in by Simon Magus? Philip had had enormous success in Samaria. There had developed a striking spiritual awakening and Samaria was no easy mission field. The Jews loathed this mongrel people called the Samaritans and, even more, that temple on Mount Gerizim rival to that at Jerusalem. But none of this blunted the power of Philip's ministry; high and low in the place hung on his words, and perhaps the biggest fish of all in the bag was Simon Magus. Philip sent word to Jerusalem to inform the apostles of all that was taking place and they dispatched Peter and John, the two foremost of their number, to see for themselves. And they, convinced that what they witnessed was genuine, laid their hands on those who had been baptized, and they received the Holy Spirit.

All this Simon watched, his eyes all but 'popping out' (as we say). What new power was this? A simple hand-laying ceremony and lo! power was transferred. At least that is how it appeared to Simon. He adored power. And whatever reality or lack of reality there was in his own profession of belief in the Gospel of Christ and his subsequent baptism it was the power he saw which filled his vision. Oh to possess that power! And then an even more unworthy thought—he might even be able to sell it! So he hurried home, scraped some hard cash into a bag and presented himself before Peter and John, the apostolic delegates from the church at Jerusalem.

I wonder if some artist has painted this picture, an artist of the stature of Rembrandt. Look into the faces of these three men; Simon's oozing with confidence and cunning, Peter's and John's faces blazing with fury, especially Peter's, for he was a powerfully emotional man. And between Simon and the apostles a bag of money being slid across the table. What words did Simon employ to accompany the cash? Were they: 'I have seen the crowds you people draw, more than I can attract—I'll give you that—How is it done? What is the secret? Give me the "gen".' And pushing the clinking coin bag a little closer did he add, 'there are plenty more like this if . . .'?

3. The Church's constant temptation

And you are thinking, Why tell us this story? We, in this congregation, are not likely to attempt to buy religious power. We aren't in Simon Magus's shoes and never will be. No, but you could pose the same question to St Luke. Why did *he* include this story in his account of the Acts of the Apostles? He could easily have omitted it if it weren't all that important. He had other material in plenty. I will suggest why—because the Church is ever in danger of forgetting that its power lies not in whatever possessions may belong to it, whether of impressive buildings, cultural achievements, intellectualism, or even beneficial social action but only in its possession of the Spirit of Christ, and *that* is not for purchase.

Please do not misunderstand this. There is nothing wrong with a church maintaining a splendid organ, worshipping with superb music, looking up to a finely crenellated spire—a landmark for the whole neighbourhood, and social activity imaginatively organized to relieve the needy. But it is impossible to purchase *spiritual power* with these or any other commodity. Spiritual power is as likely to be evident in some aesthetically barren conventicle as under perpendicular arches with light filtering through thirteenth-century glass if, I repeat if, the ministry in that place, pastor *and* people, is open to the dynamic Spirit of the living God. This power can only be received, it cannot be organized into existence. There is no coinage or skill by which it can be purchased. Fondly a congregation may imagine: if only we could boast a musical tradition like St Agatha's across the way, if only we were set in a commanding position like St Mark's Square, if only we could operate a twenty-four-hour coffee bar service, what a spiritual influence we would wield! Maybe—but not because you possessed any of those assets but only because people making contact with your minister and your congregation were aware that they were encountering a new dynamic—the Spirit of the living God, strong and compassionate.

Perhaps in all this there is a particularly hard lesson for clergy and ministers to learn, especially in their training and in the early stages of their public ministry. On the one hand there is the temptation not to bother with academic excellence and to discard all, or most, of those theological books once the qualifying examinations have been passed on the grounds that the Spirit and not the theological learning is the effective factor. On the other hand there is the temptation that presses on the learned minister to perfect his skills because then he cannot fail to gain a considerable following. Experience however shows that parishes staffed by leaders with university Firsts may not be more effective than those with humbler men and women in charge. The truth is spiritual power cannot be gained by the lack of effort on the part of the one group or the intense striving on the part of the other. Spiritual power is a gift from God which comes only to those who believe in God's power to work wonders, and who lay themselves open to him *with their skills and gifts*, whether slender or great, for him to employ, as he will.

Has the modern Pentecostal or Charismatic Movement a lesson to teach the Churches here, a lesson needing to be learned? The fastest growing congregations in the world today are the Pentecostal, and the movement cuts clean across ecclesiastical frontiers—Free Church, Anglican and Roman Catholic. And there are examples in plenty of individual so-called 'dead churches' breaking into life and vigour, expanding rapidly as a result of Pentecostal ministry. There are dangers, dangers of shallow emotionalism, an impatience with structures and the fostering of a kind of spiritual élitism; but where these are avoided, and wisdom and balance prevail, this looking to the Spirit to provide spiritual power is to be welcomed.

4. *The lesson from Simon*

Come back to Simon Magus pushing his money bag across the table and saying to the apostles Peter and John, 'Give me the same power too, so that when I lay hands on anyone, he will receive the Holy Spirit'. But, Simon, spiritual power is not for purchase! This however is not how Peter answered. No, he blazed forth in anger. 'You and your money' he burst out 'may come to a bad end, for thinking God's gift is for sale!' And as if this were not enough, he went on, 'You have no part nor lot in this, for you are dishonest with God. Repent of this wickedness and pray to the Lord to forgive you for imagining such a thing. I can see that you are doomed to taste the bitter fruit and wear the fetters of sin.' To say that Simon did not like this kind of straight talking would be an understatement. He crumpled up: 'Pray to the Lord for me yourselves and ask that none of the things you have spoken of may fall upon me.' Well, I expect Peter and John did pray for him, and who knows but that Simon the erstwhile charlatan did not come in the end to the point of sincere repentance.

There we must leave him traipsing back home, no doubt with his money bag in his hand, hating the thing but not without learning the message for which it stands. You can't buy spiritual power or position. You can't with money, brains or even ecclesiastical facilities organize spiritual power into existence. You can only receive it as a gift from God on bended knee. It is not for purchase.

16

THE GUIDING SPIRIT

The Spirit said to Philip, 'Go and join the carriage'.
Acts 8.29 (NEB)

Some time ago a clergyman came to see me because he did not know whether to accept the offer made to him of a certain parish. He described the place to me, on the strength of which, and of what I knew of the man himself, I advised him to turn it down. Wisely enough he consulted someone else who also advised him to turn down the offer. Next morning the clergyman sought me out again. 'I heard what you said', he began 'but I felt strongly during the night *guided* to accept the parish.' I was taken aback but commented, 'Then there is no more to be said, you must accept it'. To make sure, he went off to the other consultant with the same result. Later in the day we two consultants met privately and agreed, that think what we might about that parish, if the man felt guided by God there was nothing more to be said. So in due course he was appointed. That was some years ago. He is still there in that parish and doing well.

Now were we right to back down at once in the face of a strong conviction of guidance? Is divine guidance a reality or is it make believe? Is it perhaps an uprush from the subconscious of wishful thinking? Does God guide us ordinary mortals about our ordinary choices who try to live in the light of his care and concern for us? Does God the Holy Spirit guide? This is our subject for today.

1. *A guiding inner voice*

One of the most arresting stories in the New Testament concerning guidance is that of Philip the deacon. Not that he was a deacon as in the Catholic structure of the ordained ministry of bishops, priests and deacons, but he had been appointed with six other men to administer the early Church's relief funds. So he must have been known as level-headed, down-to-earth and business-like, the sort of sane person looked for as a treasurer. And Philip in particular would need to be judicious because of a complaint going the rounds in the Church that Greek-speaking widows were being overlooked in favour of Hebrew-speaking. So a language and a racial problem was on his hands, a touchy subject at any time. Fortunate then that Philip possessed a Greek name, as did all seven administrators. Clearly their appointment was tactful. They were also said to be 'of good reputation, full of the Spirit (note that!) and of wisdom'.

The administration was successful but another trouble arose. One of the deacons, Stephen, the most able of them all, in a daring speech so provoked the religious establishment in Jerusalem that a violent persecution was pursued. As a result men, women and children could be seen taking to the roads to escape arrest and imprisonment. Thus Philip found himself across the frontier in Samaria. So no more office work for him, no more allocating of funds, no more placating of disgruntled Greek-speaking widows. But being 'full of the Spirit and of wisdom' (the two are almost synonymous in the Bible) he, completely free of racial prejudice, began proclaiming Christ to the *Samaritans*. What is more, the power of the Holy Spirit was clearly with him. As the New English Bible expresses the event (Acts 8.6) 'the crowds, to a man, listened eagerly to what Philip said' and remarkable cases of physical and psychological healing ensued. All this by Philip, a layman, conspicuous in the first place for his down-to-earth administrative talents. Yet there never was such an evangelistic mission as Philip found himself conducting in Samaria. The unmolested apostles back in Jerusalem were uneasy when they heard. *Samaritans* accepting the gospel of Jesus Christ! What next? So in their uncertainty they dispatched Peter and John, the chiefest among them, to investigate. And when they saw for themselves they were convinced of the genuineness of all that was taking place and took back the good news to Jerusalem.

And then it happened, or didn't it? An extraordinary experience of guidance. Philip heard himself guided by God, as by a voice within, to break off his successful mission in Samaria to journey down to the dreary road that leads from Jerusalem to Gaza, a desert of a place. The action seemed crazy. No one can evangelize in a desert, not even Philip, not even a man full of the Holy Spirit and of wisdom. See him there squatting by the side of that apparently God-forsaken desert track wondering what on earth he was supposed to be doing in such a place. Would not wisdom counsel him to hurry back to Samaria to the eager crowds hanging on his words? But then, in the distance, there appeared a swirl of dust, stirred up by a carriage. Inside sat an official returning from a visit to Jerusalem to his court in Ethiopia and reading, mystified, the book of the prophet Isaiah. In a flash Philip knew why he was there. He had to join that Ethiopian in his carriage and feed into his enquiring mind the gospel of the Lord Jesus Christ. And wonder of wonders, the man accepted. What is more, he asked for immediate baptism which Philip administered. Then he went his way. So did the Ethiopian carrying the gospel to his own black people back in Africa. And Philip—this level-headed man—as he watched the dust envelop the chariot on its homeward way, knew that the guidance he had received was not nonsense after all. There was a strategy behind it.

So does God the Holy Spirit guide those who put themselves in his hands? Can we really trust him?

2. *Guidance by opportunities*

I want to answer *Yes* to these questions, not only on the basis of this scriptural story and others like it but from my own experience, pedestrian as it is in comparison. God does guide us as by a voice within telling us what to do, but such occasions are few and far between, and we must not trade on them lest we fall victims to spiritual pride if not fanaticism. There are however other ways by which God guides, and it is the work of the Holy Spirit to assist us to recognize them.

So I come to guidance by opportunities. Here is a man unfortunately out of work for some months, a most disheartening, perhaps even personality-disintegrating experience. But there comes on to his horizon a job training scheme. Maybe it is not what he would have liked but he is exercised whether or not to apply. What I want to say is this—that opportunity could be, I said '*could be*', God guiding that man by an opportunity, and he is more likely to accept if he is open to the concept of God's guidance in life.

Here is a teenager with a year to spare between school-leaving and university entrance. How shall she spend it? Just at the very time she is free a terrible famine smites East Africa and there is an appeal for

72

help in relief work. She could offer at the cost of abandoning a comfortable life at home. That opportunity could be God's guidance, I said '*could be*', for her. But will she recognize guidance in that form?

I admit that to accept such an understanding of divine guidance—guidance by opportunities—requires also a belief in providence. That is to say a recognition that words like 'chance', 'coincidence' and 'fate' are not the only explanations of why events happen as they do, if indeed they are ever the proper explanation. If, however, there is a providential ordering of this world, and God really is the Lord of life, is it all that surprising that he sometimes guides us by the opportunities he has made to open up before us? We may not recognize them, more is the pity, but we probably will if our lives are led consciously or unconsciously by the Holy Spirit of God; for it is his work to make us sensitive to God's ways.

3. *Guidance by Spirit-filled people*

God guides then by an inner voice, he guides by opportunities providentially provided. Thirdly—and to this now we come—he also shows us the way we should go by providing guides to whom we may, or may not, pay attention.

The Bible, not least the Old Testament, is full of illustrations of this principle. To begin with there are the patriarchs in the book of Genesis. Abraham, Isaac, Jacob and Joseph, four men of faith calling us to observe faith in God as the way of successful living; then there was Moses providing for the nation of Israel laws to govern conduct and keep it safe; then there were the prophets standing by the kings and by the common people, never ceasing to encourage them, and to warn them to keep hold of the life-style entrusted to them. All these, especially the prophets were Spirit-filled men and as such were called out by God to be his guides. And Jesus was, is, the Spirit-filled guide uniquely. His Sermon on the Mount, his parables, indeed all his teaching is meant for our guidance.

And all this, written down in the Bible, makes the Bible God's guide for us. Not that the words of the Bible are inspired as words; but the people of whom it tells were inspired by the Holy Spirit of God to be what they were, and do what they did and to say what they said. The Bible is in a class by itself as our guide; and whatever

73

guidance may come to us from other men and women, even our own contemporaries, for God still guides by calling out Spirit-filled men and women for this ministry, what they provide cannot be God's guidance if it is in flat contradiction to the revelation of the mind and will of God made known to us in Jesus Christ.

God guides then; sometimes by an inner voice (as it were) in our spirits, sometimes by means of opportunities occurring just at the right moment, sometimes by Spirit-filled people who act as God's guides. All this is true but we may write off the inner voice as wishful thinking, the sudden opportunity as mere coincidence, and the Bible as an outdated religious classic. But the man or woman in whom God the Holy Spirit dwells through faith in the risen Christ will recognize the finger of God pointing the way. Philip the deacon did this when the Spirit said to him 'Go and join the carriage'. The results were impressive. They usually are when we allow ourselves to be guided by God the Holy Spirit.

17

DOORS CLOSED BY THE SPIRIT

They travelled through the Phrygian and Galatian region, because they were prevented by the Holy Spirit from delivering the message in the province of Asia; and when they approached the Mysian border they tried to enter Bithynia; but the Spirit of Jesus would not allow them. Acts 16.6, 7 (NEB)

Closed doors then! Keep out! This is surprising. The Holy Spirit, here called the Spirit of Jesus (we shall come to that), firmly shutting doors in Paul's face on his second preaching tour. We don't think of the Spirit of God erecting road blocks. What is more, the story Luke tells in his book called 'The Acts of the Apostles' is one of steady progress on the part of the Church's mission; it doesn't lead us to expect blockages. But here in the Phrygian and Galatian region the Spirit of God said 'No' to Paul; and when he and his companions reached the Mysian border and actually attempted to enter Bithynia the Spirit said 'No' again. Paul never was a man to take kindly to having his plans checked, and on this journey to turn left and preach in the cities, notably Ephesus, towards the sea must have seemed eminently reasonable, but no, he was blocked by the Spirit. And journeying onwards to turn right and work in Bithynia for a while must have appeared common sense, but no, he was not to turn left *or* right, he was to travel straight on up towards the coast at Troas. But why? His intention in those forbidden places was worthy enough. It was to preach the gospel. So Paul and his companions experienced what some of us have had to face—closed doors.

1. Our experiences of closed doors

Will you forgive me if I recount a little story about myself? When I was about sixteen years of age I was thrilled by the two large volumes on the life and work of Hudson Taylor the founder of the China

Inland Mission, and longed to be a missionary, especially in China. I wasn't the first young Christian to be attracted by the romantic vision of living in a foreign land, living hard like an explorer and liberating people with the Christian gospel. So I made contact with the headquarters of the China Inland Mission in London, and to my surprise the candidates' secretary wrote to say he would shortly be visiting the seaside resort close to my home, for a short holiday; would I meet him? Indeed I would, this appeared hopeful. I began to see myself in China, dressed in Chinese clothing and speaking Chinese! We met, and he walked me up and down the sea front. He asked me what church I attended, what books about the Mission I had read and what was my school examination record. I told him, especially the latter because I was rather proud of it, there were distinctions. Then we parted. A few days later I received a letter turning me down. So I never became a missionary. The door was firmly shut, and as far as that avenue of Christian service is concerned, it has never been opened even ajar.

Maybe you have never had an experience quite like this but I would be surprised if you told me you had never come up against a closed door. It is a hurting experience especially if it comes with the conviction that what was hoped for was eminently suitable and right. What we have to learn, is that God guides, the Holy Spirit guides by means of closed doors as well as open ones. In this narrative in the Acts of the Apostles about Paul, Silas and Timothy what became clear through the incidence of the closed doors into Phrygia, Galatia and Bithynia was God's plan for the Christian Church to be rooted in Europe. So Paul was hedged in to press on to Troas, cross the sea to Samothrace and begin work in Philippi, a Roman city of first importance. What we are slow to learn (we cannot speak for Paul) is that God sees further than we can see, he can see the end from the beginning, he can see our end from our beginning, and there are better things in store for us than there would have been through the doors that he firmly shut. If we believe in the Holy Spirit as the guide we must believe this.

Here is another story, this time about a young woman who entered a Christian training college hoping that this would lead to useful service somewhere to which she could devote her life. She completed the course with exemplary conduct attaining first place in most of the examinations. But when the time came to leave, the staff let her know that they could not suggest any post for which she was suitable. So the door was firmly closed on all her plans, and remained closed for years. Then she married, and her particular style and manner fitted in admirably to the level of society in which she was called to live as an active Christian. So did God guide by closed doors?

No, we cannot track down beforehand the way the Spirit of God will guide, and we shall not always *see* how closed doors have always turned out for the best but when we reach road blocks in our life's journey we can save ourselves from falling into despair or resentment by remembering this experience of St Paul on his second preaching tour. The closed door in Phrygia led to the open door at Philippi and Greece and Europe beyond.

2. Bereavement—a hurting closed door

I want to touch now on the most hurting closed door of all, and I do so with great reserve. I refer to bereavement. There is no ease before the closed door of death, but more likely strained faces and tears. It is the tightness of the closure which is so hurting. Whether it has been suddenly slammed as in an accident or slowly closed as at the end of a long illness, the fact that there is no possibility of its re-opening, is the terror of this door—its finality—and the heart emptiness of those who stand by, and can only stand by, is the devastating consequence. Yes, to comfort ourselves we sometimes attempt to rationalize the parting; for sometimes it is possible to see how the closed door of death was for the best in those terminal cases where only bare existence could be the outcome of living on. 'He/she would have hated losing his/her independence' we say. But the hurt drags on. We have to live now in front of that closed door knowing that we shall not enjoy that companionship again. 'The Lord gave, and the Lord hath taken away', and whoever has loved and lost finds the standard refrain all but impossible. 'Blessed be the name of the Lord.' The closed door haunts.

I say all this although I believe firmly in the life to come; and the Church is committed to that belief, let there be no mistake. There is therefore a sense in which even the closed door of death leads on to something far better beyond it. This is why we do well not to omit some note of triumph even in our funeral service because Christ burst open the closed door of death *for us*. This is the positive message Easter signals to us. But to plan a funeral service as if it were a festival, abjuring all mourning, is bizarre. True the Christian need not fear death; let him not be blamed however if he is a little afraid of dying for no one knows exactly what it is like till he comes up to it; and bear with him patiently if he is a broken man for quite a time before the closed door which occasions his bereavement, for the hurt is his knowledge that he can never open it, no one can.

3. *The Spirit of Jesus*

Let me leave this subject and turn to something very different. In our text there stands a quite unique phrase—'the Spirit of Jesus'. Listen to the sentence where it comes. '. . . and when they approached the Mysian border they tried to enter Bithynia; but the *Spirit of Jesus* would not allow them'.

It is very easy in our thinking about the Spirit of God, the Holy Spirit, to be satisfied with the idea of a spiritual influence. A good man or a good woman is able to exercise a spiritual influence over someone else, indeed over a whole community to their lasting benefit. I could bear personal testimony to the reality of this in my own experience. So works of art—painting, music, sculpture—do actually lift those who allow themselves to be addressed by them to levels far beyond the mere material. What is more, these spiritual influences not only enhance character, they restrain it. They close doors on the trashy and tawdry. For all the authenticity of this spiritual influence, however, this is not what we are told prevented Paul from entering Bithynia. It was the Spirit of Jesus.

So Luke rooted the experience of God as Holy Spirit in the Man whom people encountered in Galilee and Judaea. There is always a danger that we shall drift away from the Jesus of history and settle ourselves with the Christ of experience. Was it not to save the early Church from this that the gospels were written? Of course we must know Jesus at a far deeper and more personal level than as a *mere* figure in the historical past. Of course we must experience the living Christ in our praying, our worship and our sacraments, but we must never allow our spirituality to be so spiritual that it drifts away from knowing or learning and following what the Man of Galilee did and said. The Holy Spirit is the Spirit of Jesus, the historical Man.

Come back to our central theme—closed doors. Did Jesus know

about closed doors in his experience? But was not the innkeeper's door closed against him in Bethlehem—in a sense he was shut out from birth. And later in Galilean society did not the synagogue doors come to be closed against him so that he was forced to preach in the open air? And as his ministry wore on were not the authorities both civil and ecclesiastical bent on closing in upon him? How did he react? Was it with bitterness, resentment and rebellion? We shall be wise when we come up to closed doors in our own experience, as sooner or later we shall, to remember the Spirit of Jesus and accept what is. The Holy Spirit sometimes guides by closed doors as well as open ones, but always to a good end. We must believe this.

18

IGNORANT OF THE HOLY SPIRIT

. . . 'we have not even heard that there is a Holy Spirit.'
Acts 19.2 (NEB)

Every now and again the question is raised as to whether or not
Britain can properly be described today as a Christian country. It is
raised because of the shocks we repeatedly register on account of the
vandalism, violence and sheer viciousness so frequently reported in
the press, which bring the whole subject of law and order into
prominence. And Church congregations are declining, fewer and
fewer young men are coming forward for ordination, and some
members of Parliament (mistakenly I think) have stated that the
Church of England as we know it will be no more in twenty years'
time. When, however, a Gallup poll is taken the surprising result is
reported that something like 75 per cent of the population in Britain
professes to believe in God. What is more, the general public clearly
accepts the traditional values and behaviour as proper—otherwise
there would not be the shock that there is over the glaring lapses.
And who will doubt the fund of goodwill and compassion that quickly
comes to the fore in Britain at any time of calamity? The money rolls
in. So is Britain a Christian country?

1. *Twelve men in Ephesus*

I see it from a religious point of view as very like twelve men St Paul
found in Ephesus, a thriving city in what we now call Asia Minor
dedicated to the worship of the heathen goddess Diana. These twelve
men stood out from the general run of Ephesians on account of the
uprightness of their way of life. They were serious, thoughtful men
who saw how little inner satisfaction the looseness and licentiousness
of the current pagan worship brought. They were upright men, men
to be relied on, men of achievement. There are large numbers of men

and women of similar stature in Britain today, they are the backbone of the nation. What is more because of them Britain cannot be labelled a corrupt society, although there is corruption in it, nor a heathen or even wholly secular society. Post-Christian? Possibly. I do not know; but not bad and not good, but respectable, respectable on the whole.

St Paul found twelve men like this in Ephesus and he talked to them, talked about their religious experience. What would you expect? And it came out that they were disciples or followers of John the Baptist. If they had actually been baptized by him in the river Jordan, it is to be wondered how they came to be living in Ephesus; but Jews of course travelled the length and breadth of the Roman empire in the interest of trade. There was quite a colony in Rome itself. Or could it be that many of those who were baptized by John in the Jordan river never did transfer their allegiance to Jesus as the Christ (which is what John intended); they observed, and they propagated John's religion of moral reform just as it was? And people joined this movement, and groups representing it were to be found widely dispersed across the Empire. There was one such group in Ephesus and St Paul discovered it.

How I would love to have been a fly on the wall when this meeting took place. Paul quizzing those twelve men. Hey! Who are you? Where do you come from? Why are you not worshippers of the Greek goddess Diana like everyone else in Ephesus? Do you perhaps attend the synagogue here? or maybe the lecture hall of Tyrannus nearby? And failing then to reach the heart of their peculiarity he put a straight, indeed a personal question, hoping to place them, as we say. 'Did you receive the Holy Spirit when you became believers?' And then I guess they looked nonplussed. Each one in the group hoped someone else would answer, because quite frankly they were out of their depth, they did not know what he was talking about. Then someone spoke up, 'No, we have never even heard that there is a Holy Spirit'.

2. *The secret of vital religion*

I hope I may be wrong, but I doubt it: my guess is that there are thousands and thousands of people in Britain today who would be bound to answer similarly: 'We did not even know that there is a Holy

Spirit.' Good people, responsible people, even religious people, maybe church-going. They would fumble awkwardly if any conversation turned in the direction of the Holy Spirit. O yes, it is a name in an ecclesiatical formula, but no more, and of no practical consequence.

So what constitutes their religion? It is being honest and straightforward, not fiddling their income tax returns or any other financial transaction. It is doing an honest day's work and playing fair with both employer and employee. No exploiting, no sweat shops, no grinding down of the poor. Religion is supporting all that is decent and uplifting, the home and family, good causes, showing compassion. Churchgoing too, has an important place, especially at the great festivals, and money gifts for church maintenance. All these things are a duty, and even if they pall there must be perseverance with them. Discipline makes the best of what is admittedly our problematical human existence, and increases the hope of survival beyond the grave, especially if there is a sincere admission of our many failures with attempts courageously made to stand up and walk uprightly again.

Well, let us be fair. It is more than possible to do business with people like this. You know where you are. They won't let you down. What a pity that more do not rise to this standard! This, however, is the searching question. Does this summary come anywhere near the heart of the Christian religion? Is there no more to it than moralism?—no more than duty and discipline? no more than patient slogging against odds? Is this all there is? Yes, it is all there is—

unless,   unless   and unless

Jesus Christ is a reality, crucified and risen, and not a figure of the imagination. Then the whole scene is changed and religion acquires an inner dynamic, a life-giving experience, buoyant and outreaching. Why? Because the Spirit of Christ, who is the Holy Spirit, has entered in through the gate of faith in Jesus. So it becomes clear why Paul pressed the question as he did to the twelve men in Ephesus, 'Did you receive the Holy Spirit when you became believers?'

Let us hear the whole incident now as St Luke set it out in the Acts of the Apostles, chapter 19. 'Did you receive the Holy Spirit when you became believers?' 'No', they replied, 'we have not even heard that there is a Holy Spirit.' He said, 'Then what baptism were you given?' 'John's baptism', they answered. Paul then said, 'The baptism that John gave you was a baptism in token of repentance, and he told the people to put their trust in one who was to come after him, that is, in Jesus'. On hearing this they were baptized into the name of the Lord Jesus; and when Paul had laid his hands on them, the Holy Spirit came upon them.

So everything turns not simply on repentance and a better way of living but on faith in Jesus as Lord at the centre. This is what makes the vital difference in religion, and I mean vital; religion with the Spirit of Christ at its controlling heart bringing new life.

John Wesley, the founder of the Methodist Church, once told this story. He dreamed that he had died and was on his way to the life eternal. In so doing he was confronted by a mighty portal and asked, 'Is this heaven?'—'No, it is hell!' came the answer. Taken aback he asked a further question, 'Are there any members of the Church of England here?'—'Yes, very many!'—'Baptists too?'—'Very many'. Then Wesley thought of his own Church: 'Are there also Methodists here?' Again there came back the astonishing answer, 'Yes, very many'. Horrified, he hurried to the gate of heaven.

Anxiously he enquired, 'Are there any Methodists in heaven?'— 'No, not a single one'—'Lutherans then?'—'No, none'—'But maybe members of the Reformed Church or Baptists?'—'No, not a single one!' Thoroughly shocked he cried out, 'What kind of people are there in heaven then?' Then he heard the answer, 'Here there are only poor sinners who through the blood of the Saviour have been made clean'.

As I said a moment ago, everything of ultimate importance in religion turns on our faith in Christ the Saviour, and this is what gives it vitality.

3. *The proper work of the Church*

I come back to where I began with the question, Is Britain a Christian country today? In a way, Yes it is, but in a way, No, it is not. In the community as a whole Christianity is fudged. We continually confuse it with moralism. Of course standards of behaviour are important. Of course law and order is important, of course personal discipline is important. No one will achieve very much in life without it. Unless, however, we attend to the spring of Christianity which is Christ, the Spirit of Christ, who is the Holy Spirit, our religion will die on us, and make no real impression on the community at large, or even our local circle.

It is just here that the proper work of the Church lies—to evoke faith in Christ and his Spirit as the way of life. The instruments for this task are the Church's worship, its rites and its ceremonies, also its preaching and teaching, but chiefest of all the quality of people it nourishes.

In November 1987 there was reported in the daily press the kind of story that rarely receives publicity. It was about a Sister Hampson, Head of St Mary's Senior School in Folkestone. What was impressive about her was her availability to help any or all in any kind of doubt or distress, herself forgotten. It was a way of life shown when she was a student at the Royal Academy of Music in London during the 'blitz', 1939–40, working in college by day and driving an ambulance by night. Then she joined the WAAF and became the first woman officer to fly into the Zone of Berlin as the war ended in 1945, having already been at hand for the Rhine crossings and the Arnhem landings, responsible, too, for loading aircraft with supplies as the BEF advanced through Europe. Six months after demobilization she felt called to become a nun in Normandy, and then after a career in teaching, housing welfare and management she became the Reverend Mother of St Mary's School in Folkestone. When she retired in 1987 the Leas Cliff Hall was crowded for her farewell party. Here was a woman singularly attractive for her sheer goodness. It was difficult not to believe that the Spirit of Christ dwelt in her. To express the matter crudely, Sister Hampson had got hold of the real thing in religion, or more accurately she had allowed the real thing to get hold of her, and that is none other than the Holy Spirit of God.

19

THE BIBLE AND THE HOLY SPIRIT

For the word of God is alive and active.   Hebrews 4.12 (NEB)

My subject today is the Bible and the Holy Spirit. Put like that it sounds (to non-specialists like ourselves) abstract, theological and remote from our everyday concerns. We can hardly pay attention. This is a pity because the Bible need not be boring, indeed will not be boring, but alive, active and challenging if it becomes the word of God to us. To make it so is the work of the Holy Spirit; or to put the matter another way, it is the Holy Spirit who makes the Bible become the word of God. This is what I invite you to think about now.

1. *A human book about God*

(*a*) Let us begin at the beginning. First of all, men wrote the Bible—not God. It did not fall down from heaven, nor was it dictated by God. What is more, the writers used all the human skills of which they were capable, just like any other writer. Listen to St Luke, the author of the third gospel. 'Many writers have undertaken to draw up an account of the events that have happened among us, following the traditions handed down to us by the original eyewitnesses and servants of the Gospel. And so I in my turn, your Excellency, as one who has gone over the whole course of these events in detail, have decided to write a connected narrative for you, so as to give you authentic knowledge about the matter of which you have been informed.' Nothing here about God whispering truths into St Luke's mind so that he could write the gospel! All the emphasis is upon the trouble he had taken to produce the most authentic account possible. So with the whole Bible. It is a humanly produced document and therefore not faultless, nothing human ever is, but it is substantially reliable—the various authors worked to make it so.

(*b*) But is the Bible inspired? Yes, of course it is inspired. The writers were inspired when they wrote it. All great writing is inspired and the Bible is great writing, perhaps unequalled writing for where will you find anything to match the twenty-third Psalm or 1 Corinthians 13, St Paul's hymn to love? If you doubt this estimate of the quality of the Bible as literature, listen to some of the recordings of the late Lord Olivier reading it. And like all inspired writing it reaches out to realities beyond the circumstances of its times, and maybe beyond all time. The Bible cannot fail to be classified as Grade One in the whole realm of literature.

(c) Still we have not reached the heart of the matter. The Bible is not uniquely treasured simply because it contains a generally reliable account of the origin and rise of the nation of Israel, the ministry of Jesus, and the growth of the Christian Church. Neither its history, nor its literary merit contains the secret, but something else. The Bible is different because it is a book *about people's experience of God*; no, not men and women's ideas about God, but about God acting in creation, in history and in the course of people's lives, and what we can deduce about God from these actions of his. No wonder then the Bible consists largely of stories about events that happened. It is not a theological treatise.

(d) When we think like this about the Bible we can see how great is the material in it for *learned studies*—history, language, textual criticism, literary criticism, ancient customs and cultures; no wonder research students have found more than enough to occupy their scholarly skills down the centuries. But is the significance of the Bible to be discovered by the application of learned intelligence? The answer must be No, which is not to say that all their academic Bible studies are valueless, or are to be set aside, far from it. They are illuminating. They add enormously to our appreciation of the Bible and to our understanding, but they do not constitute the reason for the place the Bible holds in the Christian Church and why she claims it as her book.

2. *A book able to become the word of God*

Here then is the answer; we prize the Bible because it has the potentiality to become *the word of God* to us, and when it does we may know that the Holy Spirit of God is at work operating between the printed page, or the voice of the reader, and he or she who is consciously attending to it. And when the Bible becomes the word of God it is no longer dull or boring, it is alive and active. It cuts more keenly than any two-edged sword, piercing as far as the place where life and spirit, joints and marrow, divide. It sifts the purposes and thoughts of the heart! So Hebrews, chapter 4, verse 12.

And now I am out of my depth as I so often find myself to be in trying to preach. I have to confess I simply do not know why it is that the Bible has the potentiality to become the word of God in a way to which nothing else can begin to compare. I have also to confess I do not know why it is that the Holy Spirit of God uses this book above all others to bring us into touch with God in a kind of personal encounter. It simply is a fact to which a multitude of witnesses could be called to testify.

I remember noticing a middle-aged man creep into one of my congregations when I was a vicar and sitting behind a pillar. The service was Evensong and the set lesson the story of the Prodigal Son in Luke 15 which I read. What could be more ordinary? Then I preached on it. That too was ordinary. But for that man that summer evening that scripture became the word of God. It drove him to make contact with me, to tell me how he had not attended a church for thirty years, to confess that he had risen high in his profession and was decorated for it, was well-to-do, but his wife had died some months previously leaving him alone, wretched and miserable; he felt utterly unable to face life much longer. But God as a concerned and caring heavenly Father became utterly real to him as he sat behind that pillar during Evensong, and the experience saved him from disintegration, enabling him to make a new life. I know because I kept in touch with him for the rest of his life.

This is why we treasure the Bible—because through it we can hear a word of God addressed to us personally where we are. The Holy Spirit is at work as interpreter in the congregation of worshipping Christians to make this possible.

3. Preaching from the Bible

It is in this context that preaching is to be understood. All proper preaching is Biblical preaching. It is opening up the Scriptures by a preacher on whom the Holy Spirit of God rests, using all the skills and learning of which he is capable so that those Scriptures may become the word of God to the hearers. Preaching is not indoctrination, neither is it emotional manipulation, it is helping the members of the congregation *to see God at work*, and in particular to see Christ who is called the Word of God and so to know God, for the way to that knowledge is through him. It is the work of the Holy Spirit of God to reveal Christ as he himself said according to John 16.14: 'He shall glorify me: for he shall take of mine and shall declare it unto you.'

When I was a vicar in the West End of London I recall an occasion when I startled my somewhat sophisticated congregation by claiming to be a window cleaner, a window cleaner in the pulpit. Until I explained I sensed that the members were a little abashed at their vicar's humble calling. But, as I pointed out, I was not there to regulate their behaviour nor to indoctrinate them with orthodoxy or the latest unorthodoxy, I was there to help them *see more clearly* God at work in the world and in their own circumstances and to employ the Bible stories as a means of doing it. My responsibility was to help remove whatever obscured their vision of God. I was in fact a kind of window cleaner, no more no less.

4. *Three instructions for reading the Bible*

Now if all this is true that the real significance of the Bible is that it can become the word of God to us wherever we are and no matter how diverse our needs, then at least three practical conclusions follow. The first is that we should treat it with respect. No small part of the offence caused by some of our modern radicals is that they almost 'rubbish' (if I may use that contemporary slang word) those parts of the Bible they find difficult. Of course there are difficulties. Of course alternative solutions to the orthodox may be suggested, but it is wrong to write off any part of the Scriptures as unworthy of the attention of intelligent men and women.

Secondly, Bible reading needs to be preceded and followed by prayer. Prayer in order to realize the presence of God. Prayer for the opening of the eyes of the spirit on to what is being read. Prayer too that the word of God may be heard speaking to us through the words of the Scriptures.

Thirdly, as well as being read in private, couched in private prayer, the Bible needs to be read in the worshipping community, congregation or group. This is because when two or three are gathered together in Christ's name, his Spirit, who is the Holy Spirit is present and active and he it is who makes the Bible become the word of God.

5. *A book to be experienced*

I come back to where I began when I announced that my subject was to be the Bible and the Holy Spirit. For all the trouble I have taken to make it plain, I have to admit that the idea of the Bible becoming the word of God to us by the power of the Holy Spirit can only be given any countenance at all through experiencing it. The situation is not unlike what I encountered some years ago in Switzerland. My wife and I were sitting on the deck of one of those little steamers that used to ply between Interlaken and Thun on Lake Thun (and possibly still do). The clouds hung low over the mountains and none of the glories of the scenery we were hoping to see were visible, making all of us passengers miserable. Suddenly a Frenchman rose to his feet, pointing with outstretched arms and hands and shouting '*Regardez, Regardez*'. And we did, all of us. We stood up and looked, and there was the Jungfrau, completely free of cloud, its snow cap a brilliant pink caught by the setting sun. Now try as I may, arranging my words this way and that, I cannot convey to you the wonder of suddenly seeing a glory we least expected. It is only possible through experience. So with the Bible becoming the living word of God addressing our very souls. It can only be known through experience.

20

THE SPIRIT, THE FELLOWSHIP AND THE SACRAMENTS

'Repent', said Peter, 'repent and be baptized, every one of you, in the name of Jesus the Messiah for the forgiveness of your sins; and you will receive the gift of the Holy Spirit.' Acts 2.38 (NEB)

I ought to preach an ecclesiastical sermon. Of course I ought. Pentecost marks the birthday of the Christian Church. And if I sound reluctant it is only because I know how deadening, indeed apparently irrelevant, ecclesiastical structures can sound to most ordinary people if given the priority over spiritual experience. Pentecost is primarily about the *experience* of God, not law and order, no, not even order. Yet ecclesiastical structures there have to be—otherwise we may lose the benefits of spiritual experience. So be patient, be patient with rites, regulations and rubrics. They mean well!

1. *The fellowship*

Let me begin by reminding you what basically the Church is—it is the fellowship of the Spirit. It is the coming together, and staying together, and even seeking to increase the number of those people whose lives the Spirit of Christ has touched, and who allow it to operate in what they think, and feel and do. The spirit in the fellowship, because it is the Spirit of Christ, is the distinctive fact about the Church. Without that spirit it has no real *raison d'être*. And when anyone has contact with the Church, either in its worship or its outreaching this is the spirit which must be felt. So we hold *together* the Church and spiritual experience and do not allow them to be an either/or; and if this is what is meant by saying that a healthy faith is one that is both evangelical and catholic, it cannot be wrong.

Now the fellowship in which is the Spirit of Christ is the Church's primary evangelizing agency. And when the Church is weak, and when the distinctive spirit within its fellowship is weak it makes little or no impact on the community at large or on individuals who encounter it. At times we have to admit that it is weak, more is the pity, then divisive issues take over and the Church becomes more ineffective still. What impresses about the early days of the Church's life after Pentecost is the description St Luke gives of it in Acts 2.46: 'With one mind they kept up their daily attendance at the temple, and, breaking bread in private houses, shared their meals with unaffected joy, as they praised God and enjoyed the favour of the whole people.'

'With one mind.' Yes the unity of the Church is fundamental. Primarily it is a unity of the Spirit, for the Church is the fellowship of the Spirit. To *construct* this unity by means of theological formulae and regulations is not possible. It is a unity of the Spirit and special care is needed not to destroy what unity of the Spirit there is *across* ecclesiastical boundaries. For let us not forget—not that we are in much danger of doing so—ecclesiastical boundaries do exist, some more unsurmountable than others. We cannot simply shake off our history. And if modern schemes of reunion are slow to succeed, and a good deal of enthusiasm seems to have gone out of them, let us be thankful that today there is more unity in the Spirit across the ecclesiastical boundaries than there was yesterday. Yes, even in Northern Ireland! Neither let us forget that *uniformity* in Church life may not be desirable because a uniform Church in a nation can easily become a domineering Church, and then it loses its compassion.

There is a practical conclusion to all this. Where Churches in one place can act together they should do so but without destroying or compromising the distinctive life of each. Perhaps the most straight-forward area is in social and relief work. And there can be no doubt that where this takes place it does much to commend and reinforce the gospel of Christ. There can also be occasions when different denominations can worship together. Intercommunion is more diffi-cult. There are those who see intercommunion as the way *to unity*, others who see unity as the necessary stage *before* intercommunion. If I may express a personal view, and it is no more than that, I would prefer that an attitude of occasional hospitality no more, no less, be adopted by the differing denominations and that we should be con-tent with this till guidance for the future is more clear. I see this as nourishing the unity of the Spirit which is the fundamental.

91

Strengthen the fellowship then, the fellowship of the Spirit and see that the spirit in the congregation is its distinctive feature, something even the newcomer will sense.

2. *Baptism*

And now baptism, one of the two sacraments of the gospel. The word 'sacrament' puzzles some people. It is not a word in every day use. We don't hear it on the train or in the bus queue. Never mind the Latin origin, basically a sacrament is a material thing standing for an experience. A ring stands for a marriage. It signifies it. You can't see or touch marriage but you can a ring. So the visible and tangible stands for the invisible and intangible. Since therefore the spiritual realities with which the Church deals are neither visible nor tangible, it is not surprising that it employs sacraments, the one to stand for, or signify, the other. So sacraments are signs of spiritual realities; they are more, they are places where the Spirit of God *operates*, that is to say they are effective signs. A parallel to this is the kiss between a man and a woman. It indicates love (at least we hope so!) but it does more, it stirs up love. It is an effective sign. And putting out a flag on Armistice Day indicates the existence of patriotism, and even advances it somewhat; at least we should doubt its future if no flags appeared. Baptism and Holy Communion, then, are sacraments of the gospel, they are rites where the Spirit of God is at work reaching out to us.

So baptism. It signifies new life in Christ, new life come about by responding to the word of the gospel—which is Christ crucified and risen for us and in whom we have the forgiveness of sins and the promise of eternal life. This new life is enacted sacramentally in baptism, that is to say it is an effective sign of it; and it introduces the one baptized into the fellowship of the Spirit, namely the Church where the distinctive spirit is *caught*, and growth in the Spirit is nourished.

All this is easier to follow in the case of adult baptism, following on the experience of conversion, which is the situation reflected in the New Testament. We have, however, infant baptism. This points to the more common means by which those of us who are Christians have become Christians. It is by nurture in the faith rather than by conversion from outside it. In our cases (notice, I include myself), baptism, and certainly the confirmation of that baptism in the rite that bears the name, introduced us into the life of the Church, which is the fellowship of the Spirit, and there the Spirit of Christ took hold of us.

So baptism is an effective sign of the work of the Holy Spirit and always the Spirit calls for the response of our spirits.

3. *The Holy Communion*

And now thirdly, the Holy Communion or Eucharist. This is the central act of worship of the fellowship of the Spirit, the Church. There has been something of a revival of Eucharistic worship in the Anglican Church during the last half-century, and even more emphasis upon it than formerly in Protestant Churches generally. Undoubtedly it has become a more meaningful act of worship for many, though it would be hard to deny that the Eucharist has in some cases, in being popularized, become little more than a sacrament of *fellowship*. A celebration at every kind of gathering together, and not always for worship, can lead to a reduction of what the Eucharist essentially is—namely, the mode in which the Holy Spirit maintains the presence of Christ himself in the fellowship, and in the individual lives of the baptized who constitute it. Baptism then is the effective sign, the sacrament, of the call of the Holy Spirit into the fellowship of the Spirit, the Church; the Eucharist is the sacrament of the Holy Spirit's nourishing of that fellowship, and its individual members by the body and blood of Christ. Where exactly the Spirit works in respect of the bread and wine in the Eucharist is a matter of differing opinions not to say controversy. This is reflected in Rite A of the Alternative Service Book. In the first three Eucharistic Prayers the President prays 'grant that, by the power of your Holy Spirit . . . these your gifts of bread and wine may be to us the body and blood . . .', whereas in the fourth Eucharistic prayer the emphasis is on the reception of the elements and not on the elements themselves. 'Grant that by the power of your Holy Spirit we who receive these gifts . . . may be partakers of his most blessed body and blood.' Hair splitting! you say. Well, not in Church history down the centuries! But we shall be wise not to let the difference of opinion destroy the fellowship of the Spirit which is the essence of the Church's life and especially at this most sacred point. Let us be alive to the presence of

Christ in the Eucharist by the power of the Spirit and be nourished and refreshed in our spirits thereby.

I fancy I can hear someone heaving a heavy sigh over all this. What has it to do with facing life tomorrow at the office, or bearing with a painful illness, or facing up to retirement? Well, I said I was going to preach an ecclesiastical sermon and I have! And I have overstepped my text from Acts 2.38: 'Repent', said Peter, 'repent and be baptized, every one of you, in the name of Jesus the Messiah for the forgiveness of your sins; and you will receive the gift of the Holy Spirit.' But in speaking of the fellowship, baptism and the Holy Communion I have not strayed from the context in which my text occurs. The Holy Spirit does operate in those three places, which is why they have special significance in the life of the Church and must not be neglected. Let us then try to understand them.

21

OUR BODIES AND THE HOLY SPIRIT

Or know ye not that your body is a sanctuary of the Holy Spirit which is in you? 1 Corinthians 6.19 (RV marg)

I admit I am not bursting to preach this sermon, indeed to assert that I am reluctant to preach it would be nearer the truth; and if I were a *visiting* preacher in a church I certainly would not preach it. If however I omitted from my preaching on God the Holy Spirit *as a whole* any reference whatsoever to behaviour, and sexual behaviour at that, and adhered solely to theology, I could be charged with distorting the balance of the New Testament and particularly the letters of St Paul, for St Paul consistently devoted the first half of his letters to doctrine and the second half to ethics. This is my point—the subject I am to handle today is proper in *the context* of a whole and balanced Christian ministry, but not in isolation. Furthermore it is undeniably only proper for me in that context because I have neither expert qualifications, nor wide experience to attempt counselling on sexual problems. I do however claim to be a life-long student of the New Testament and am therefore not without some sort of right to preach one sermon (anyway) on the Holy Spirit as his indwelling governs the sexual conduct of those who call themselves Christians. Let me repeat my text—it is not the only one along this line in the New Testament—'know ye not that your bodies are a sanctuary of the Holy Spirit which is in you?'.

1. *The despised body*

Now I propose setting out three attitudes to sexual behaviour, and the first is that which was current in the world where the early Church grew up and the New Testament took shape.

In so far as serious thought was given at all to the relationship of the human spirit to the human body, the body was looked upon as the prison house of the soul. To appreciate how this idea gained currency is not difficult. Who is there who does not know from experience how our nobler aspirations—and we have them—too often become thwarted by the demands of the body, be they laziness, appetites or plain weakness and illness, in fact all that pertains to our mortality. So the soul is the good part of us, the essentially independent good part, the part ultimately destined for immortality when the body is no more; but, and this is the human tragedy, it is constantly being dragged down by the body. So the body is a corrupting thing, even a worthless thing, except for the passing pleasure it provides in this life. What can be wrong therefore with indulging it according to personal preference though exercising care, possibly, to avoid excess? At the end of the day the body will count for nothing, it will disappear in dust and ashes; no outright condemnation therefore attaches to sexual licence in itself. This was the thinking in the Greek-speaking world where the early Church led by St Paul, and the apostles, preached the gospel of Jesus Christ. Not an easy climate, you must admit.

2. Sex—a physical function

And now, secondly, the climate of thought in our modern Western world. It does not of course build on the ancient Greek philosophical basis, and it is to be wondered how many people even in that ancient world paid conscious attention to it; for the most part they probably simply surrendered to their appetites. Nevertheless in that old world sex was seen to carry a certain mystery, if not awesomeness about it, evoking a kind of reverence—after all did it not in a god-like way even produce life? So various taboos and initiation ceremonies were attached to it as is the case even in primitive cultures. Not surprisingly therefore there was held to be a certain sacredness about sex labelled by writers on the subject as *sacral*.

This sacral acceptance of sex has entirely disappeared in contemporary Western culture, indeed to employ the word 'sacred' in reference to sex would sound comic to modern men and women. Nowadays sex is widely regarded as essentially a pleasurable bodily function to be exploited as such; and people deprived of it are unfulfilled if not stunted personalities. Freudian psychology and the contraceptive pill have largely contributed to this outlook. One result however is to make sex meaningless beyond being a function of the body with emotional overtones not dissimilar to eating and drinking. Not surprisingly therefore a variety of manuals has proliferated on modern bookstalls, and presumably in sex shops, on how to obtain the maximum pleasure from sex, suggesting a variety of methods as in tennis, swimming or golf in order to improve technique. And clearly, since sex has now become a technique, the part played by romantic love is minimal and all but discounted. All in all then, sex is popularized as something everybody does, and in progressive circles arrangements for cohabitation are made as readily as for a dinner appointment. Sex is a way of getting to know people and to acquire partners as in a pleasurable pastime.

This is progress. This is liberation. Anyway, this is the theory. What I have described is not quite the whole picture. Some groups in the modern secularized world have taken the matter a stage further. They have promoted sex to the stature of functioning as an index of political and social liberation achieved. In such circles new members are required to establish their membership by first of all losing their virginity; indeed deliberately to rebel against conventional/sexual morality is to show oneself a true revolutionary over against the Establishment. This is reckoned to give sex a meaning in the modern world of sex technique.

The modern view of sex is not so much advocated as assumed, making conventional morality, which still exists, live uneasily beside it. Its essence is to regard sex as primarily a physical function to be enjoyed as opportunity and desire afford with no disapproaval attached.

3. *The Christian understanding of the body*

We turn now to the New Testament understanding of sex pinpointed in St Paul's letter to the Christians in Corinth, 1 Corinthians 6.19: 'Know ye not that your bodies are a sanctuary of the Holy Spirit which is in you?'

How different this sounded from the prevailing view of sex in Corinth where the recipients of this letter lived. Nothing here about the body being a prison of the soul. Nothing here about the body being despicable and destined for dust and ashes anyway, and therefore able to be indulged with impunity. Instead, 'know ye not that your bodies are a sanctuary of the Holy Spirit?' How did the Corinthian Christians receive it? Corinth was a sink of iniquity. The city was actually dedicated to the worship of Aphrodite the goddess of lust, whose temple boasted a thousand courtesans euphemistically so-called. Moreover because of its geographical situation it was a highwāy for the commercial traffic passing from west to east and east to west. Here in Corinth, Rome, Greece and the Orient all met and mingled, and the Corinthians, a showy, talkative, argumentative people, loved it. They were out to drink the cup of life to the full giving rise to the phrase 'to live like a Corinthian'. Corinth was like the great seaports the world over. You pay your money and you get what you want, especially down the back streets.

The marvel is some of these Corinthians actually believed the gospel of the risen Christ and God the Holy Spirit operated in their subsequent lives, but St Paul, the preacher of the gospel to them, and the founder of the Church there, had his 'work cut out' (as we say), to lead them away from the current sexual looseness. They argued along the lines to which they were accustomed: that the body is designed for the intake of food and drink and actually requires them for life let alone pleasure; so is it designed for sex, therefore to supply the need cannot be wrong. It was in this area of personal conduct that St Paul had some of the hardest battles to fight in his Churches. But don't miss the point! He did fight them. The conduct of Christians in sexual matters is meant to be different. Because everyone is loose is no argument for the Christian to be loose, even in Corinth. 'Know ye not that your bodies are a sanctuary of the Holy Spirit which is in you?' Christians must be different.

The nub of the matter is our attitude to our bodies. In Corinth as elsewhere in that ancient Greek culture the body was given a low rating. In our modern culture it is given an exceedingly high rating but they are similar in one respect that any consideration of the effect of the body on the soul is negligible. It is just here that the Christian sex discipline cuts a straight line across. 'Know ye not that your bodies are a sanctuary of the Holy Spirit which is in you?'

The Christian view is not of the body and the soul as two separate entities. A person is a body–soul complex. The *personality* of each one of us is affected by his or her body, and the *body* of each one of us is affected by his or her personality. Physical sexual union therefore has consequences for the personality or soul. This is why the

Christian cannot regard as a matter of indifference who sleeps with who. The Christian gospel is concerned for souls and *bodies*, bodies and *souls*. It must therefore require a different code of practice in sexual relationships on the part of those who claim to be Christians. A policy of *laissez-faire* or 'anything goes' is contrary to the gospel.

Is this hard? Of course it is hard. It was hard for the Christians in Corinth, and in Thessalonica and in Rome, or why did St Paul have to deal with it in his letters to all three places? But the Christian is not unfortified. 'Know ye not that your bodies are a sanctuary of the Holy Spirit which is in you?' The Holy Spirit imparts to the Christian strength to stand, even to stand out, in his temptations and subsequent conduct, as the Lord Christ did himself when tested in the wilderness after his baptism. But do not forget this. These Corinthian Christians had not always been, never were, entirely 'oil paintings'. They had fallen and they fell again, or some of them did. Yet if they repented, there was always forgiveness and restoration. The Church in Corinth, and the Churches throughout the world was/are composed of forgiven and restored sinners, not saints from birth. Don't forget this, but don't forget either how our bodies are rated in the light of the Christian gospel. 'Know ye not that your bodies are a sanctuary of the Holy Spirit which is in you?' We must be different in our Christian conduct.

22

TWO HOUSES

For we know that if the earthly frame that houses us today should be demolished, we possess a building which God has provided— a house not made by human hands, eternal, and in heaven.
2 Corinthians 5.1 (NEB)

Rather more than thirty years ago my wife and I received a legacy. It was small, insufficient today to purchase even a 'mini' motor car but at the time when we received it we were able to buy a very modest house in the country with quite a large garden. So we had a 'second home', that is to say a place in addition to the vicarage we occupied. And it gave us a certain peace of mind. Should one of us die there would be this house where the one left could live; and if we both lived into retirement, there it would be ready to accommodate us—which in fact is what has happened. Yes, we were fortunate. I admit it. Some clergy today are trying to do likewise, but it is not so easy with the modern high cost of housing.

Two houses then. This is what our text is about except that they are not houses of bricks and mortar in this world, but one on earth—our bodily frame, and one in heaven. 'For we know that if the earthly frame that houses us today should be demolished, we possess a building which God has provided—a house not made by human hands, eternal, and in heaven.' The Lutheran Bible uses two different words for these houses, the first it labels *diese Hütte*, this hut or cottage; the second *einen Bau*, a building, construction or edifice.

1. *Our first house*

We think then of our first house, 'the earthly frame that houses us today'. Maybe it is only a cottage in comparison with that 'not made by human hands' which shall be, but how we love it! and how right we are to love it! It comprises all that we experience with our five senses and with our minds, a wonderful world full of fascination, interest and beauty. How few are the people who long to leave it, how normal it is for us all to cling to it, loath to let it go, anxious to prolong our life in it to the last breath, straining all the resources of medical science to do so. How the doctors tried with General Franco and the Emperor Hirohito!

And this earthly life of ours can be wonderfully good and was meant by God the creator to be. Does not the Bible picture him after each creative act as pronouncing it 'very good'? How warped in judgement are they who can see no beauty around them, hear no music, never rock with laughter and for whom all food and drink tastes alike, men and women whose hearts love has never warmed nor success ever elated! But what is far more sad, people whose lives have been so hemmed in, so starved, so deprived perhaps by illness or misfortune or the wickedness of oppressors, that they have scarcely ever seen the sun—slum dwellers, slaves, prisoners, the permanently hospitalized, broken people, deprived people, all the little crushed and unwanted beings of this world—yet even they cling to the little they have. And here is something remarkable, those who have been hit hard by what has happened to them are sometimes more aware of the second house not made by human hands that is to come; suffering sometimes, not always, clears the vision, often it depraves.

All of which leads me on to make this point. It is no part of proper Christianity to neglect this first house. We are to enjoy it and never to cease from helping those less fortunate than we are to enjoy it too. We cannot be indifferent to social welfare. But we are not to be 'worldly', by which I mean we are not to be trapped into thinking that only this world, and our enjoyable life in it is all that matters. It can be a trap. This-worldliness runs down into emptiness and at the end inner dissatisfaction in which is no joy. Curious as it may sound, the only way to make the most of this 'earthly frame that houses us today' is to believe that when it is 'demolished we possess a building which God has provided—a house not made by human hands, eternal, and in heaven'. Christians then are people who know they possess two houses.

2. *Our second house*

And now I come to our second house, to one 'not made by human hands, eternal, and in heaven'. I have been reading the newspaper about those unhappy people who on account of the recent rise in interest rates find themselves faced with mortgage payments they cannot meet and are in consequence homeless. They have nowhere to go. I cannot think of any situation more disturbing. Homelessness 'knocks the bottom out of life'. What our text affirms is that this will not be our case when we quit, through death, the earthly frame that houses us today, on the contrary we possess a building God has provided. We have a second house.

So we are not, after death, consigned to a vague kind of existence as a ghost, spirit or shade wandering about in nothingness. Whoever is united to Christ does not die into an emptiness, a kind of unfeeling nothingness, he is not condemned to an endless soul wandering, which is the impression some religions seem to give. God will raise us up to give each one a new body, not this present body reconstructed, but a body corresponding and fit for the new world of God's eternity. Let me repeat, we do not go out into nothingness but to our second 'house not made by human hands, eternal and in heaven'.

3. *The pledge*

But how do we know? How do we know we have a fullness of life beyond the grave and not a pale wraith-like reflection of this? If we read on in 2 Corinthians, chapter 5 from verse 1, which constituted our text, to verse 5 we shall receive the answer. I quote, 'God himself has shaped us for this very end; and as a pledge of it has given us the Spirit'. That word Spirit is written with a capital S, the reference is to God the Holy Spirit. The gift of the Holy Spirit now is the pledge of heaven to come.

I think we need to sit back for a moment and 'take this in'. That some men and women possess a spiritual awareness is surely evident. We might not rank them all as saints (in the popular understanding of that word) though some are. But there are people who are aware of God's presence, who radiate goodness, who achieve results in their lives far beyond the average, people of a dynamic faith. Of these it must be said that the Spirit of God rests upon them. The quality of their lives is not the product of their own striving but a gift from God, it is the Spirit of Christ operating in them. But why? To make their life more comfortable? It may do just the reverse! To make it more acceptable to the community at large? But such people are often despised if not persecuted! Why then?—Because we are made for eternity, we are not made for dust and ashes as our final destiny. And that some people are spiritual now is the pledge that a *spiritual destiny* is God's purpose for all of us; and for fear we might interpret it in ghost-like terms we read in St Paul's letter to the Corinthians that we are to possess a *building*, a *house* not made by human hands, eternal and in heaven.

I invite you to think of Churches in this light. They are communities of the Spirit, they are there and they hold together because the Spirit operates in them. As such they witness *beyond themselves*. No, not primarily to moral standards, to a distinctive way of life or even to values, that 'in word' of the present age, though all these are characteristics; rather they point away to the eternal world, to that which is beyond the here and now and all that is temporary and passing. This is why a church building which houses the living Church is most appropriately constructed with a spire pointing upwards to the heavens. That is where we ultimately belong, that is our destination, our second house 'not made by human hands'. The Spirit we have received now is the pledge or guarantee of this.

O yes, I know, we long for more details. When you have lost someone whose life was closely bound up with yours so that you can even guess what they would be thinking, and who was always so active, you cannot imagine what they have been doing in that other world where they have gone since they left us through the gate of death. Did Jesus in Galilee and Judaea know? He came from the realms of glory. But he did not tell us. Did he know after he was risen from the grave on Easter Day and appeared to his disciples even talking to them? But he didn't say. So we must conclude that while we live in our first house we could not begin to appreciate what life could be like in the second house even if we were told. But we can trust. We have the pledge of God the Holy Spirit. And we can love. All of which, perhaps, is summed up nowhere more beautifully than in the Prayer Book Collect for the Sixth Sunday after Trinity, 'O God, who hast prepared for them that love thee such good things as pass man's understanding: Pour into our hearts such love toward thee, that we, loving thee above all things, may obtain thy promises, which exceed all that we can desire; through Jesus Christ our Lord. Amen.'

23

TEST THE SPIRITS

... No one can say 'Jesus is Lord' except by the Holy Spirit.
1 Corinthians 12.3 (RSV)

1. Who is a Christian?

I wonder how you would define a Christian? A man or woman who is consistently kind and charitable?—and of course a Christian should be—but are not many others of no religious faith kind and charitable?, and yet others who adhere to another religion altogether, say Buddhism or Hinduism? Surely this definition will not suffice, it is far too general. Then there is the other extreme, the demand for an exclusive acceptance of *every phrase* of the Apostles' Creed, and as if this were not enough, subscription to the Thirty-Nine Articles of the Book of Common Prayer, even belief in the verbal inspiration of the Bible. But this is far and away too narrow.

Over against this excessive breadth and this excessive narrowness the early Church had a clear-cut way of deciding who was a Christian—anyone ready publicly to make the confession 'Jesus is Lord'. The Roman persecutors of the Christians knew this, which is why in the correspondence between the Roman emperor Trajan and Pliny the Younger, governor of the province of Bithynia (date AD 112) we can read of how anyone suspected of being a Christian was put to the test with one question 'Are you willing to curse Christ?' If they did so there and then they were set free, if not they paid the price often with their lives, notwithstanding how law abiding they might be in every other respect. All of which means that the three words in our text 'Jesus is Lord' are nothing like as simple as they sound. They are decisive words, definitive words, they tell in the matter of belief who is a Christian and who is not.

Maybe, however, you are not convinced. The words 'Jesus is Lord' sound simple enough to you. But are they? *'Jesus is Lord.'*

Note where the accent falls: *Jesus* is Lord. They were, there always have been and still are, people who profess to be Christian but who virtually dispense with Jesus, the man of Galilee. Their adherence is to what they call the 'Christ-spirit'. They might be learned radical theologians, perhaps in German universities, who make a sharp divide between the Jesus of history and the Christ of faith; it is the latter that is decisive, not the former. They might on the other hand be what, for the want of a better title, could be called 'super spiritually minded' people. Provided we have the mind of Christ, they say, and live in his Spirit nothing else matters, not even the substantial reliability of the story of Jesus as told in the gospels, all this can be let go, it belongs, if anywhere, to the elementary and therefore dispensable early stages of faith. Some of these advocates appeal (wrongly I think) to a text in 2 Corinthians 5.16, 17: 'Even though we have known Christ after the flesh, yet now we know him no more. Therefore if any man is in Christ, he is a new creature'—this is all that matters.

2. The touchstone of our faith

(a) The historical Jesus
Our text however is definite—*Jesus* is Lord. Let me quote the context in full (NEB).

> You know how, in the days when you were still pagan, you were swept off to those dumb heathen gods, however you happened to be led. For this reason I must impress upon you that no one who says 'A curse on Jesus!' can be speaking under the influence of the Spirit of God. And no one can say '*Jesus* is Lord!' except under the influence of the Holy Spirit.

And this emphasis on Jesus, the historical man, as a keystone in Christian faith is further emphasized in 1 John 4.1-3:

> But do not trust any and every spirit, my friends; test the spirits, to see whether they are from God, for among those who have gone out into the world there are many prophets falsely inspired. This is how we may recognize the Spirit of God: every spirit which acknowledges that Jesus Christ has come in the flesh is from God, and every spirit which does not thus acknowledge Jesus is not from God.

So '*Jesus* is Lord', He is the touchstone of our faith.

(b) *The risen Christ*

And now the second word in the trio. 'Jesus is Lord.' Not, you will notice, 'Jesus *was* Lord'. This use of the present tense carries with it the confession that Jesus lives. 'Jesus *is* Lord.' It implies the resurrection. All of which means that a Christian is not one who simply agrees that Jesus is an historical figure, and a notable one at that, a teacher whose insights and precepts deserve the closest attention, even to the extent of seeking to live by them, Jesus being in himself a striking example of what he taught. And that he accepted crucifixion rather than surrender to what he held most dear makes Jesus a martyr for truth on the noblest of scales. What further elevation, what additional accolade, you might think, could be accorded him? Have we not in all this what constitutes the heart of the Christian faith? And the answer is No, splendid as it may sound, and in some ways is; the basic confession is: 'Jesus *is* Lord'. The Man of Nazareth *is*, not *was*. He lives now. He rose from the dead, He is risen.

The reference then to the resurrection is not *simply* to history, though it is that. It is not satisfying ourselves that the tomb was empty on Easter Day where Jesus had been buried and that he was seen by Mary Magdalene, and others after he was risen, it means that we can be *in communion with him now*. That is to say a Christian is one who has spiritual communion with Jesus. He lives in his presence though he cannot be consciously aware of it all his time occupied as he must be with many other activities.

(c) *The Sovereign Lord*

And now the third word. 'Jesus is *Lord*.' Here again we have a depth not apparent perhaps on the surface. Jesus as the man of Galilee and Judaea was sometimes called 'Lord' by those who were impressed by his works and his words, the phrase being more or less equivalent to the way we use 'Sir' as a mark of respect. The first title, however, accorded him which was more than a mark of respect was 'Christ'. In calling Jesus by the title 'Christ' recognition was being made that he was God's agent in the world, the one through whom supremely God was carrying out his purposes for mankind. The resurrection stamped this title on Jesus. He was known as Jesus Christ. Yet even this was not the sum total of understanding about Jesus. He came to be called Lord, so that his full designation is 'The Lord Jesus Christ'. This accords him sovereignty. He is Lord over all the world. He is to be worshipped. In his presence the head is to be bowed. With the creator of all that is he is divine.

This supreme confession, 'Jesus is Lord', has far-reaching ethical consequences. If Jesus is Lord, if he is 'my Lord', how should I go about my own life? And how is he to be Lord in the world as we know it? What social action is required making possible the realization of Jesus as Lord in an ever changing environment? It is not too much to assert that the confession 'Jesus is Lord' is a revolutionary one. Taken seriously it changes commonly accepted standards and customs. If Jesus is Lord how can slavery, torture, deprivation and a hundred other cruelties ever be tolerated? The consequences of the confession 'Jesus is Lord' are indeed immense.

3. *The work of the Holy Spirit*

Come back to the text 'No one can say "Jesus is Lord" except by the Holy Spirit'. What does this mean? It means no one can come to the point of making this profound confession about Jesus as Lord by a process of logical reasoning. It is not possible to prove that Jesus *is*. It is not possible to prove that he rose from the grave on Easter morning. It is not possible logically to work out that Christ is now risen and that he is God's agent in the world. And as for Jesus being the Lord this is not intellectually demonstrable, which does not mean that it is unintelligent. How is it then that down through the centuries in many different lands and cultures Jesus has been and still is worshipped as Lord? Have they, have we all been duped? Is blind sentiment or emotionalism the reason behind the Church's worship of the Lord Jesus Christ? Or is it—and here I come to the crux of the whole matter—is it that the Holy Spirit of God has been, still is and always will be at work among peoples the world over, opening the eyes to see who Jesus is? The Spirit of God operates supremely, but by no means exclusively *in the Church*, that is the company of believers in Jesus, and the Spirit is caught there. This is the *experience* (please note) by means of which men, women and children are brought to the confessional stance—'Jesus is Lord'.

And is this not true to your experience? You did not work out your Christian stance by a process of reasoning. Nor did I. We caught *the*

Spirit first of all from our home upbringing, from our Church, some group or even one person who influenced us. We cannot boast about our faith. We caught it or it caught us. All this because the Holy Spirit was at work. 'No one can say "Jesus is Lord", except by the Holy Spirit.'

24

THE FELLOWSHIP OF THE HOLY SPIRIT

The grace of the Lord Jesus Christ and the love of God and the fellowship of the Holy Spirit be with you all. 2 Corinthians 13.14 (RSV)

In the course of the last three or four years I have accepted an invitation on more than one occasion to preach to the German Lutheran congregation at the Marienkirche in London. I felt a little strange at first although I am not unfamiliar with the German language. In spite of the many differences between Anglican and Lutheran worship, I soon felt at home, and especially in the 'get together' after the service. I recognized at once the distinctive feature wherever people who believe in Christ meet each other—a strange warmth, understanding and caring, based on mutual acceptance. This of course is due to the Spirit of Jesus in whose name the contacts are made. What is being actualized is the communion or fellowship of the Holy Spirit, language and cultural differences notwithstanding.

There are, of course, all manner of gatherings together of people besides Church in the world, each with some distinctive concern, object or interest—be it scientific, recreational, educational or political; but however deeply I might share one of those interests I could not help wondering as I left the Marienkirche if I could ever have sensed belonging as I did there had I attended those other meetings, especially if all the participants had been German. Is not this the truth? The Spirit of Jesus in a group creates a distinctive kind of fellowship because it is the fellowship or communion of the Holy Spirit.

Now the text I have chosen to end this book of sermons on the Holy Spirit is really a benediction: 'The grace of the Lord Jesus Christ and the love of God and the fellowship of the Holy Spirit be with you all.' St Paul was using it to bring to an end his letter to the Christians in Corinth labelled in our New Testament '2 Corinthians'.

He did not have an easy time in Corinth. The inhabitants of that city were notoriously noisy, obstreperous and flamboyant; and when they became Christians they were still more than a little 'difficult'. Not only did some of them flaunt their disobedience to the Christian life-style: they loudly questioned the authority of the apostle himself. How significant then that he should end his letter with this benediction 'the fellowship of the Holy Spirit be with you all'.

1. *The grace of the Lord Jesus Christ*

How then does this distinctive fellowship come about whether in Corinth, in the Marienkirche in London or St Agatha's Parish Church deep in the country? It starts with the grace of the Lord Jesus Christ. First of all there has to be acceptance of what we owe to him. We do not begin with the love of God. We begin with Jesus. The love of God is not obvious. Ask a mother who has lost her baby in a cot death. Ask the bereaved man whose wife did not escape when the train on which she was travelling crashed. Ask the flood victims of Bangladesh. Ask the rape victim on one of London's streets. Yes, there are glorious aspects of this world, breathtakingly glorious. I think May in England displays a panorama of them. And God is the Creator! Yes, but there are puzzles, enigmas and huge hurting questions; perhaps the existence of pain and suffering twists itself into the most ugly. No man, no woman who is sensitive can with ease believe in the love of God looking at his creation as we know it. I have to confess that I do not think I could go on believing in God at all were it not for Christ, Christ tortured and dying cruelly on the cross. I could not believe in God if he created the world and then (please excuse the crudity of expression here), and then sat up in heaven and dodged the horrible aspects of it all. I have to believe that God was in Christ, in Christ on the public gibbet, going down into hell—interpret that as you will—or I simply have no faith in God whatsoever, no use for God. And when I ask, as I have asked, Why did he become incarnate in Jesus? why did he stoop to this awfulness? it must have been because he so loved us, so loved us that he cares for us to believe in him since without that faith we lose our way in earth's strange pilgrimage. All this is what we call grace, the grace of the Lord Jesus Christ, the gift—please note, gift, of himself to save us from becoming lost in the fog of uncertainty over God's enigmatic creation.

Where then does the fellowship, the communion of the Holy Spirit begin? It begins in gratitude for Jesus Christ—the baby in the manger, the teacher and healer of Galilee, the tortured victim of human wickedness on the cross, the risen Christ from the grave. You cannot manufacture your faith with any tools or techniques, nor can I. We have to believe in what is *given*, freely given, namely the ministry of the Lord Jesus Christ.

2. *The love of God*

And now, secondly, 'the love of God . . . be with you all'. What does this mean? Basically God's love for us made known in Jesus Christ, but derived from it our love for God, so the mutual love between God and ourselves, ours being a responding love.

What a difference love makes! I was talking to a primary school teacher the other day in one of our big Midland cities, and she suddenly said, 'Of course you cannot enjoy any success as a teacher unless you love the children. Without this little progress will be made whatever changes are made in the syllabus. This is where some recruits to the profession lose their enthusiasm for it. They do not really care for the children.'

We all know how in the absence of love, mutual love, a marriage can turn sour. So can life in the absence of any awareness of the love of God. Bitterness can creep in on account of the raw deal life seems to have handed out to us. We may, in consequence, go about with a permanent grudge, or what is sometimes called 'a chip on the shoulder'. It matters little in this situation what advantages, possessions, or opportunities are afforded, grounds for complaint will always be found, and there will be resultant poor performance. Of course there are difficulties, set-backs, and frustrations to be found in life, some almost heart-breaking. Very few of us escape them altogether, and those who do, or appear to, are not usually the people who make a significant success of life. Great people are people who have triumphed over great difficulties but they would never have done so had resentment bitten hard into the core of their being.

Here is a man born with one leg shorter than the other. A small matter, you may say, but from the time he was unable to take part in the normal school games his deformity has dogged him. But he won the love of an understanding woman, and in his love of her, and hers

111

for him, he has succeeded in life where many more fit than he have grumbled all the way.

No wonder then Paul put the love of God into his benediction for the Corinthians. Difficult though they were, he wished them well and he knew nothing more likely to bring this about than an awareness of the love of God outstripping, and finally conquering, their innate quarrelsomeness and rebelliousness. They could be, they would be, a warm-hearted community.

3. *The fellowship of the Holy Spirit*

And now the fellowship of the Holy Spirit. Paul longed for this to be enjoyed by the recipients of his letter. 'The fellowship of the Holy Spirit be with you all.' Do any of us need a reminder of what a comforting, strengthening, even inspiring experience fellowship can be? We thirst for it. Loneliness is a slow killer. We all need the support of others. I expect this is true even of those who become known as 'loners', even sailing round the world solo. Always at the back of every life is some other person, some group of persons. We are made for fellowship and cannot live without it. To this the very first book of the Bible bears witness in the Creation story. God said 'It is not good that man should be alone, I will make an help meet for him'.

And when at Pentecost the Holy Spirit brought life to the newborn Church the fellowship of the members was one of the characteristics that marked it out, a warm, caring, boundary-crossing fellowship. In such an atmosphere great work is possible, even miracles. No wonder Paul in his benediction wished for the fellowship of the Holy Spirit to be realized in practice among the Corinthians.

Do I have to refer to the Greek word for the fellowship or communion used here and elsewhere in the New Testament? It is *koinōnia*. It really means sharing. The members of the early Church, we are told in the Acts of the Apostles, *shared* their possessions; they had all things in common—*koinē*. And strictly speaking when Paul wrote 'the fellowship of the Holy Spirit be with you all' he was longing for the sharing of the Holy Spirit. That is to say the Corinthian Christians sharing in the intimate bond of communion that exists in the Godhead between the Father and the Son. The Nicene Creed touches on this when it says 'the Holy Spirit proceeds from the Father and the Son'. Jesus lived in this communion in Galilee and Judaea. It was the source of his insight and power. He was the Man of the Spirit. Through the Spirit he shared the Godhead.

And now I am at the end of what words to use to describe this fellowship or sharing. All I can ask is whether we can enter into it, even a little way. If we can, and the way must be through the prayer of communion, then even I, unexcitable East Anglian though I am, can understand how in some Pentecostal forms of worship there is an urge to dance, clap hands and sing. The sharing of the Holy Spirit produces life, movement and enthusiasm. Who shall say we do not need this in our Churches today, especially in our Western lands? But we must not forget wisdom. Wisdom is one of the gifts of the Spirit. In our enthusiasm to show we have appropriated St Paul's benediction—'The grace of the Lord Jesus Christ and the love of God and the sharing (fellowship) of the Holy Spirit be with you all', let us also exercise wisdom lest we frighten would-be partakers away and they lose what they could gain.